50 Ways to Love Your Stepparent

Approaching the Heart with a Rational Mind

Sarah Cline, Ph.D.

Copyright © 2023 Sarah Cline, Ph.D.

All rights reserved.

The contents of this book may not be reproduced, duplicated, or transmitted without direct written permission from the author.

Under no circumstances will any legal responsibility or blame be held against the publisher for any reparation, damages, or monetary loss due to the information herein, either directly or indirectly.

Legal Notice:

This book is copyright-protected. This is only for personal use. You cannot amend, distribute, sell, use, quote, or paraphrase any part of the content within this book without the consent of the author.

Disclaimer Notice:

Please note the information contained within this document is for educational and entertainment purposes only. Every attempt has been made to provide accurate, up-to-date, and reliable complete information. No warranties of any kind are expressed or implied. Readers acknowledge that the author is not engaging in the rendering of legal, financial, medical, or professional advice. The content of this book has been derived from various sources. Please consult a licensed professional before attempting any techniques outlined in this book.

By reading this document, the reader agrees that under no circumstances is the author responsible for any losses, direct or indirect, which are incurred as a result of the use of the information contained within this document, including, but not limited to, errors, omissions, or inaccuracies.

ISBN: 978-1-937209-20-9

Contents

Introduction ... 1
   Learning about Personality Types
   First Thing First

1. Understanding Personality Types: A Deep Dive ... 3
   Origins of Personality Types
   Cave Dweller (CD) and Mountain Yeller (MY)
   Key Takeaways

2. Communication Is Everything ... 17
   Express Feelings Without Instigating Conflicts
   Prioritize Active Listening
   Use Neutral Language to Curb Defensiveness
   Communicate Dynamics and Expectations
   Establish Open Communication
   Deal with Unresolved Issues from Your Biological Parents
   Attend Family Counseling if Necessary
   Schedule Personal Time for Reflection and Understanding
   Share Personal Growth Moments
   Respect Their Space and Yours
   Key Takeaways

3. Try to Level Emotionally ... 35

Talk to Them
Don't Wait for Them to Take the Lead
Offer Surprise Gestures
Organize Family Get-Togethers
Include Them
Write Them Letters
Offer to Help Them
Key Takeaways

4. Celebrate the Dynamic   52
Invite Them Over for Dinner
Celebrate Your Parent and Stepparent's Anniversary
Create Memory Gifts
Celebrate Them "Just Because"
Thank Them for Doing Their Best
Remember Them on Father's Day and Mother's Day
Recognize Their Achievements and Yours—Together
Share Life-Altering Moments with Them (Even the Bad Ones)
Tell Them You Love Them
Create Traditions
Key Takeaways

5. Appreciate Them for Who They Are   62
Celebrate Their Emotional Strengths
Get to Know Their Personality Types and Love Languages
Show Interest in Their Past Before They Became a Stepparent
Show Gratitude for the Relationship You Have with Them
Become Their Friend
Key Takeaways

6. Boundaries and Opinions   71
Set Boundaries

When You Ask Them for Advice, Respect It
Give Them the Benefit of the Doubt During Misunderstandings
Avoid Being Offensive with Your Language
Define Relationships with All Parental Figures
Key Takeaways

7. Socializing with Your Stepparent   80
Call Them
Let Them Confide in You
Show Physical Admiration and Affection
Get Together for the Holidays
Let Your Kids Call Them "Grandma" or "Grandpa"
Take Them Out
Laugh Together
Take Them on Family Vacations
Plan Game Nights and Family Get-Togethers with Them
Revisit Places of Significance
Key Takeaways

8. Final Thoughts   97
Above Everything Else, Communicate
We Are All Human
Respect Differences
Take Responsibility
Stop Making Assumptions
Stay in Contact and Practice Being Present—Even When There's Conflict

Appendices   103
Self-Assessment Questionnaire: Determine if You're a CD, MY, or Straddler

Cave Dweller Tendencies
Cave Dweller Priorities
Mountain Yeller Tendencies
Mountain Yeller Priorities

Introduction

Stepfamilies are complex and often shrouded in guilt or fear of the unknown, especially when it comes to loving our stepparents. But fear not, dear reader. Just by picking up this book, you are taking a brave first step towards understanding and enhancing your relationship with your parents and stepparents. Within these pages, we will delve into three distinct personality types that shape relationships within families and step-families alike: the reserved Cave Dweller (CD), the outgoing Mountain Yeller (MY), and the Straddler, who exhibits traits from both categories. With practical insights and real-life examples of these personality types, you will have an arsenal at your disposal to help you navigate the intricate dynamics of relationships while also gaining a deeper understanding of yourself. So, get ready to see your parents, stepparents—and perhaps even yourself—in a whole new light as we explore 50 ways to love your stepparents.

Learning about Personality Types

Buckle up, because we're about to uncover the mysteries of CDs, MYs, and Straddlers. Think of it as a personality safari, where we'll observe these fascinating creatures in their natural habitat and gain a deeper understanding of each type, as well as how they might pertain to your everyday sort of situations. Armed with this knowledge, you'll be able to decode your stepparent's behaviors like a pro and avoid any misinterpretations. No more of the blame game when it comes to misunderstandings; it's all about recognizing and respecting our inherent differences. So, let's hop on this wild ride and learn how to better connect with our loved ones.

First Thing First

Forget the quick fixes and checklists, because loving others is an active effort. This book will guide you, but it's up to you to truly apply these insights. It may require some soul-searching and challenging your current beliefs, but the payoff is worth it—a deeper bond and a better understanding of yourself and those you love. So let go of any guilt you may have for wanting to love your stepparent, or fear about the unknown, and instead embrace the process of growth.

Chapter One

Understanding Personality Types: A Deep Dive

Do you find yourself needing help understanding the personality traits of your family? Do you ever feel frustrated that they seem dissimilar to you? Or frustrated that they're so similar to yourself? What about your stepparent? Do you feel the need to understand them more?

Understanding personality types is an essential piece of the puzzle when seeking to understand others—and your stepparent is no exception to that. Appreciating them means discovering their true layers and complexities, and all of them should garner your attention if you are ever to experience a happy and healthy relationship.

In this chapter, we will discuss the personality types of the Cave Dweller, which we will refer to as CD, the Mountain Yeller or MY, and the Straddler. Learning about these three basic personality types will give you a clearer picture of the unique benefits and challenges each creates. And understanding is an essential first step to bringing harmony and happiness into your everyday life.

Origins of Personality Types

Before the modern-day classifications of CDs and Mys, and even before psychiatrists and psychologists stepped onto the scene, ancient civilizations sought to explain human behavior and its various nuances.

The Ancient Greeks

The ancient Greeks developed the theory of four humors to explain the causes of health and illness both mental and physical. This theory suggested that an individual's temperament was influenced by bodily fluids: blood (sanguine), yellow bile (choleric), black bile (melancholic), and phlegm (phlegmatic). The Greeks thought these humors were directly related to being sanguine (cheerful), choleric (short-tempered), melancholic (reserved), or phlegmatic (relaxed). Therefore, the balance of these humors was believed to influence an individual's temperament, health, and overall disposition. An imbalance of this humor led to behaviors that today we associate with certain mental illnesses. For example:

- Sanguine (blood) was associated with cheerful, optimistic, enthusiastic personality traits. An imbalance was thought to be due to a person having too much blood in their body, which would cause them to be overly confident and have impulsive behavior. Today we would think of this as possible narcissistic or bipolar disorder.

- Choleric (yellow bile) was associated with being ambitious, passionate, and easily angered. An imbalance causes anger, irritability, or extremely aggressive behavior and rage. Modern psychology would call this possible borderline personality disorder.

- Melancholic (black bile) was associated with being thoughtful, reflective, and often sad or depressed. This imbalance was associated with melancholy and depression.

- Phlegmatic (phlegm) was associated with being calm, reliable, and often unemotional or apathetic. An imbalance was associated with lethargy, sluggishness, or a lack of motivation, which, much like melancholic, is a symptom of depression.

Treating these emotional ailments is where things got even more interesting. If the Greeks thought you had an imbalance of any of these four humors, you would likely have received one of the following treatments.

Dietary Changes: Prescribed depending on the humor in excess. For instance, someone deemed overly choleric might be advised to avoid hot or spicy foods that would "agitate" the yellow bile.

Bloodletting: If you were someone believed to have an excess of sanguine humor, it was common practice to be prescribed bloodletting. This process involved removing blood from the body by way of leeches or actual cutting.

Purging: To remove excess bile or phlegm, laxatives were used, as were emetics, which induced vomiting.

Baths/Sweating: To promote toxin removal, balms, and ointments were applied to the skin to help imbalance these four humors.

The Greeks' attempts to "treat" imbalances in personality or health were based on the observations and the knowledge they had at the time. The four humors theory was eventually replaced with more accurate medical models, but its influence can still be seen in some of our language today.

The Introvert and the Extrovert

Carl Gustav Jung (1875–1961) was a Swiss psychiatrist, psychoanalyst, and the father of analytical psychology. He developed several concepts that had a profound influence on both psychology and popular culture. One of his most notable contributions was the concept of *introversion* and *extraversion* (often used in the more modern manner: introvert and extrovert). Jung's theory asserts that introversion and extraversion are attitudes that represent the direction in which a person's psychic energy flows.

Extraversion (Extrovert)

According to Jung, the extrovert's energy flows outward. This personality type is more oriented toward the external world and derives energy from interacting with its surroundings, including people, events, and situations. If your parent is an extrovert, they tend to be more outgoing, social, and interested in external events. They are typically action-oriented and more comfortable in social situations than an introverted parent. External factors influence parental extroverts, who are occasionally prone to negative introspection.

Introversion (Introvert)

As the name suggests, the introvert's energy flows inward. This personality type is more oriented toward the inner world, relying on introspection and internal reflection. If your parent(s) is (are) introverted, they are generally more reserved and often feel more comfortable with individual activities or smaller group settings. They derive energy and pleasure from thinking, daydreaming, or exploring ideas. Although an introverted person's daily practices tend to lead to social isolation, they tend to have a small number of deep connections with people of their choosing.

Jung believed that everyone has an introverted and extroverted side, with one being more dominant than the other. It's a spectrum, and while some people might be near the extremes of that spectrum, most individuals lie somewhere in between.

Cave Dweller (CD) and Mountain Yeller (MY)

While not strictly rooted in these historical contexts, the CD and MY classifications are evolved constructs reflecting the same human desire to understand ourselves and others in our world more deeply.

While our contemporary understanding of the CD and MY classifications doesn't stem directly from ancient Greek or Jungian theories, much like their historical counterparts, they are observed patterns in modern relationships. By identifying recurring patterns, we can forge tools to help us navigate and harmonize interpersonal interactions.

Cave Dweller (CD)

We must first learn about their traits to determine where you and your stepparent fall on the CD or MY scales.

Reserved Nature

If your parent is a CD, they will predominantly be calm and reserved. CDs are introspective and tend to hold their emotions close to their chest because they value their inner world and the sanctuary it provides. Their reserved nature doesn't mean that they are indifferent or don't care about those around them; it just means that they process their emotions internally and over time.

For instance, after an argument, a CD might withdraw to process their feelings rather than immediately confront an issue. A CD does this because they typically feel uncomfortable with strife and need time to work through their emotions and consider how to communicate their feelings.

Socially, a CD is often found in quieter corners engaging in deep conversation with one or two individuals rather than in the center of a party. In group discussions, a CD will offer insights only if specifically asked or if they feel strongly about a topic.

Logical Thinking and Literal Communication

A CD leans more toward analytical and logical thinking. They make decisions only after careful contemplation and weighing the pros and cons. They work hard to keep their emotions from clouding their judgment. This logical thinking manifests in their communication; they will get to the point without inserting emotions or using stories to embellish their point.

For example, if you discuss a film with a CD, they will likely dissect plot points with impeccable logic and even point out strengths and weaknesses. But they often miss the emotional undertones of the movie. If you ask a CD if they liked the cake you brought for dessert, they might reply, "Yes," without diving into flowery descriptives.

It's important to note that a CD may also get frustrated with an embellished story that takes longer to get to the point. It doesn't mean they don't want to hear the story or don't care what you have to say; their brain is just geared toward immediate outcomes.

Need for Space

A CD has an inherent need for emotional and physical personal space. For them, requiring space is not about distancing themselves from loved ones. It's about needing solitude to recharge and reflect.

CDs enjoy reading books in a cozy nook or going for solitary walks. They may listen to music while cooking dinner instead of talking. This alone time is essential for a CD, especially after a day filled with social interactions.

Singular Focus

A CD has unparalleled concentration when engrossed in a task and prefers completing that task to their satisfaction before tackling another.

If you attempt to talk to a CD while they're writing an email, for example, they may be so absorbed in what they're writing that you'll be tuned out. It's not that what you're saying is unimportant to them; it's just challenging for them to spread their focus on more than one thing at a time because they give each item their full attention.

Social Preferences

Traditionally, if your parent(s) were labeled an introvert, others would consider them anti-social. But that couldn't be farther from the truth. An introvert, or a CD, just leans toward more intimate social interactions. Large gatherings can overwhelm a CD and drain their mental and emotional battery.

Emotional Processing

While CDs might not outwardly express their emotions, they experience them *deeply*. However, their internal reflections may lead to a delay in their outward emotional expression. While a CD may seem distant after an emotional confrontation, they must process the interaction before reacting. A CD needs time to contemplate a disagreement, analyze the conversation, and figure out where things went wrong before they can move on to a resolution. This meditation is essential for a CD's family member to understand; the more you push them to express themselves, the more they will clam up in response.

Deeper Dive into the Mountain Yeller (MY)

If your parent is an extrovert, chances are they've been called that more than once in their lifetime. An extrovert is typically known for being outgoing and the life of any party. But there's so much more to them than meets the eye.

Outgoing Nature/Group Socialization

An MY is inherently outgoing. Their energy thrives on interactions and being around people as often as possible. Instead of needing time alone to recharge, MYs wants to be out and involved.

At a social event, MYs will be the first to initiate games and dancing and will often bounce from person to person, catching up rather than focusing on one task at a time. Deep conversations are still on the table, but not at a social event. An MY usually rallies their friends for a group outing over a weekend rather than sitting at home reading a book or watching TV. Even in the workplace, MYs love group projects and find collaborative brainstorming and teamwork exciting.

Emotion-Driven

MYs are heart-ruled because they lead with their intuition and emotions. Being ruled by their heart doesn't mean their decisions are devoid of logic, but their feelings heavily influence their reactions. An MY can be emotional during arguments but is also the first to send a heartfelt message to a friend or family member upon hearing they are having a rough time.

An MY's emotions will show throughout their storytelling, so be patient when they tell you about an event or relay the plot to a movie. Chances are both will be full of details and embellishments.

Connection and Touch

MYs crave genuine connections and physical touch, whether a hug, a pat on the back, or simply holding hands. It reinforces their feeling of being connected. In relating with you, an MY will crave physical affection and see it as a top priority over other needs—something we'll discuss in depth a bit later.

Dynamic Focus

An MY is a natural multitasker. Instead of focusing on one task at a time, their attention shifts between assignments. They enjoy the energy they get from juggling multiple things and often get bored working on one project for an extended period.

An MY doesn't mind dealing with paperwork but works through it while watching television or listening to music. As for conversations, an MY loves to chat, but don't be surprised if you find them scrolling on their phone while talking with you. It's not that they think what you have to say is unimportant; their mind simply runs at a faster rate than a CD, making them more comfortable processing more than one thing at a time.

Inferential Communication

An MY often communicates using stories, anecdotes, and metaphors rather than getting straight to the point. They rely on indirect implications and expect others to infer meanings, which can confuse some who aren't familiar with their communication style.

During an argument, someone may find it hard to decipher what the MY really wants, even if they feel they have told them directly. It's essential to have a middle ground where communication is concerned, especially if your parent is an MY and you are a CD, because the communication styles between personalities are very different.

Immediate Emotional Expression

Unlike their CD counterparts, MYs are quick to express their emotions. They're an open book and rarely hesitate to share their feelings of joy and disappointment. This can be overwhelming for a CD uncomfortable with an emotional display.

One of the greatest fears an MY faces is the fear of rejection. If an MY has a CD child who usually pulls away at any sign of conflict, this can be a bone of contention. An MY will take your withdrawal as a sign of personal rejection. It's important to communicate that you are not rejecting them and need time to wrap your head around and process the disagreement. Give the MY verbal and physical affirmations whenever possible.

If you are a CD and your parent is an MY, don't panic; it doesn't mean you cannot have a successful parent/child relationship. There are plenty of amazing and fulfilling relationships between opposites. It just means it will take time, work, and patience to learn one another's needs and effectively communicate.

The Straddler

If your parent is a Straddler, they are adaptable and enjoy the best of both worlds. They can immerse themselves in a book like a CD or be the life of a party like an MY. They possess an emotional agility that allows them to straddle their personality types seamlessly. While this book predominantly focuses on CD and MY, Straddlers can use it to understand the extremes and navigate their middle ground more effectively.

Excellent Balance between Reflection and Expression

A Straddler can introspect like a CD, valuing quiet moments of thought. Yet, they also appreciate the expressive vitality that an MY has and share their feelings and ideas openly when a situation calls for it. They are as happy spending a quiet evening reading and attending a book club as they are actively participating in a lively discussion.

Adaptable in Social Situations

While they might not always be the life of the party, Straddlers easily adjust to situations based on the social settings and the company involved. They can engage in a one-on-one conversation at a party and then join a group game or be at the party's center later in the evening.

Values: Both Logic and Emotion

A Straddler approaches situations with a logical mindset but is equally attuned to the emotional undercurrents, valuing the importance of feelings in decision-making. For example, if a colleague faces a personal issue, the Straddler will offer practical solutions while providing emotional support.

Flexibility in Needs and Fears

The Straddler's hierarchy of needs fluctuates based on circumstances, and they might experience the same fears from a CD's spectrum, such as loss of security, and the MY's fear of rejection. However, adaptability allows them to prioritize different aspects of their life. While working on an important business project, they will prioritize career stability, but in downtime, they will focus on relationships and personal connections.

Fluid Communication Styles

A Straddler can communicate directly and inferentially, often adjusting communication based on the recipient. For example, when conversing with an analytical boss, they will be direct and to the point, but when they talk to their best friend, they become expressive and delve into all the nitty-gritty details.

Straddlers possess an innate ability to mediate and find common ground, especially in relationships where CDs and MYs might find themselves at odds. Their adaptability enables them to comprehend and empathize with both personality types, easing communication and diminishing misunderstandings.

A Straddler may seem like the perfect personality type. However, everyone encounters their share of struggles. The flexibility of a Straddler often confuses their preferences and needs. The Straddlers might sometimes feel stretched or trapped in the middle, particularly in a polarized situation where they wish to please others so much that they struggle to voice their disagreements. A Straddler must discern what is truly significant to them while learning to navigate other personality types, much like everyone else.

So, How Do You Find Common Ground?

"I'm a CD, and my parent is an MY; is my relationship with them doomed?"

No! In this book, we don't tell you how to "cope" with differences. We allow you to realize each person's unique strengths in a relationship. A CD's introspection can balance an MY's spontaneity. A MY's vivacity and exuberance can harmonize beautifully with a CD's depth and stability.

Recognizing these different traits is merely the first step to a healthy relationship. The real challenge, and indeed the focus of this book, is to find ways to navigate the complexities of these interactions. After all, the beauty of a relationship truly unfolds in the dance between these personalities.

Key Takeaways

Diving into the intricacies of personality types isn't about affixing labels but enriching our understanding. With these insights, you're now armed with the necessary vocabulary to navigate the labyrinth of human emotions and connections, fostering an environment where love thrives, understanding blossoms, and relationships flourish. As we traverse this journey, let's remember that the goal isn't to change but to adapt, understand, and love more deeply.

The foundation for a nurturing relationship starts with understanding—understanding yourself, your stepparent, and the dynamics of your interaction with one another. With the knowledge of CD and MY personality traits, you're well on your way to deepening that understanding, setting the stage for the subsequent chapters that will guide you on how to cherish your stepparent in ways that resonate with both of you.

Understanding personality differences is essential for nurturing compatibility. This chapter has illuminated the fundamental traits of CDs, MYs, and Straddlers.

- **Reserved Nature:** Respect your CD stepparent's need for personal space and quiet reflection. Don't force immediate emotional reactions.

- **Logical Thinking:** Recognize your CD stepparent's analytical approach. Be patient as they process before expressing feelings.

- **Singular Focus:** Acknowledge that multitasking is difficult for your CD parent. Allow them to complete or pause their task before they give you their full attention.

- **Emotion-Driven:** Empathize with your MY stepparent's emotions. Give them positive affirmations/compliments and physical affection.

- **Inferential Communication:** Listen for meanings implied indirectly in your MY stepparent's stories. Learn to read between the lines.

- **Dynamic Focus:** Accept your MY stepparent's wandering attention. Multitasking is in their nature. However, if you need their full focus, tell them.

- **Excellent Balance:** Appreciate the adaptability of a Straddler but avoid putting them in the middle of conflicts.

- **Flexible Needs:** Accommodate shifts in a Straddler's priorities. Reassure them of your unconditional love.

Chapter Two

Communication Is Everything

Effective communication is the foundation of any healthy relationship, regardless of whether it is a romantic relationship, a parent/child relationship, or a relationship with your stepparent (which sometimes may be closer than a biological parent/child relationship). It also does not discriminate against personality type.

Communication is the bridge that connects us all—whether we are CDs or MYs. It enables us to come to a mutual understanding and build a stronger bond.

In this chapter, we'll delve into the essential components of communication that can strengthen the bond you have with all of your parental figures. Moreover, the chapter will navigate the traits of each personality type and how you can use personality indicators to validate your stepparent, yourself, and each of your needs.

While it's easy to be swayed by the idea that love is a mysterious force beyond our control, the reality is that maintaining a lasting relationship requires a lot more than just love. It requires conscious effort, respect, and a willingness to understand one another on a deeper level. This journey of appreciation goes beyond knowing your stepparent's favorite "things" or doing what you think will make them "happy." It's about diving deep into their psyche (and yours), comprehending their unique personality traits (and yours), and recognizing how their attributes interact with yours in a way that can formulate a healthy and lasting relationship.

In the age of digital connections and instant gratification, we sometimes forget the beauty of human interaction. We often overlook the importance of patience, reflection, and presence with our loved ones. At times, we also let external factors beyond that pull us away from what truly matters. Thus, you can pause, reflect, and feel as we progress through this chapter. By fostering an environment of open communication and mutual respect, you're not just building relationships and bonds but cultivating relationships that thrive on understanding, compassion, and genuine connection. Using this guide, you can learn how to not just communicate you're your stepparent, but these

Here are some strategies and ground rules to help you convey your emotions effectively.

Express Feelings Without Instigating Conflicts

Expressing your feelings is crucial for any relationship, but it's also essential to do so without triggering conflicts. It's too easy to get wrapped up in emotions when expressing them to someone else—especially when you're first sorting through them—so it's crucial to take a step back, breathe, and formulate thoughts before verbalizing them. This is especially true with your parents and stepparents. Sometimes tensions are high, and unfortunately, this is especially typical of blended families.

As an adult, you may think that now is the time to lay everything out on the table. While this can be true—and even beneficial for your mental wellbeing—it is important to understand how to do it healthily. Make sure to keep the heightened emotions to a minimum to avoid as much conflict as possible.

Remain Calm

Try not to overreact to difficult situations. By remaining calm, it's more likely that your stepparent will respect you enough to see your perspective.

Express Feelings with Words, Not Actions

If you start to get angry and feel you may lose control, take a break, and do something to help yourself feel calm.

- Take a walk.
- Do breathing exercises.
- Interact with a pet.
- Journal.
- Read a book.

Address One Issue at a Time

Only introduce tertiary issues once the primary problem has been fully discussed. This way, you'll avoid what experts call the "kitchen sink effect." Dr. John Mordechai Gottman (born April 26, 1942), an American psychologist and professor at the University of Washington, coined the term to describe the act of one person in a discussion or argument throwing "everything but the kitchen sink" into it by dredging up past mistakes and grievances. This tactic is particularly counterproductive, as it's often overwhelming to the person receiving the grievances.

This is especially true of your parents *and* stepparents. Even if you have childhood grievances, avoid bringing them all up during a time of argument or debate. These are better suited to planned discussions. Family therapy sessions are especially helpful in these sorts of situations.

Resist Underhandedness

Avoid hitting below the belt or being underhanded. Tensions can be high in this sort of relationship, and it may seem easy to hit below the belt when upset, but don't use conversations—or any situation—as an excuse to attack your stepparent. There are likely sensitive areas that you could easily trigger or even hurt their feelings—and although this may be tempting in the moment, avoid it. These attacks only foster distrust, anger, and harmful vulnerability. We don't want to "win" arguments. We want to work through issues by effectively communicating.

Avoid Clamming Up

Positive results can only be obtained by way of proper communication. It's easy to feel emotionally charged when discussing your feelings with your parents, and a stepparent is no exception. In fact, it may even be more emotionally charged. When emotions run high, we "clam up" or shut down often.

It's important to note that when one person becomes silent and stops responding, frustration and anger can quickly follow. If you feel overwhelmed or as though you're shutting down, you may need to take a break from the discussion. Just remember to follow up on the discussion later. Likewise, respect the fact that it may be your parents who need the space.

Be Specific and Productive

Be precise about what is bothering you. Try not to generalize. Avoid words like "never" or "always." These sweeping terms are usually inaccurate and will (almost) always heighten tensions. Instead of using hyperbole, focus on what you're feeling in the moment. Vague complaints are also challenging to address, and tackling each specific item productively is important.

Prioritize Active Listening

Practice active listening when your stepparent communicates with you. Avoid interrupting them when they're speaking, even if you disagree. Active listening is the cornerstone of all effective communication—and relationships in general. It involves not only hearing the words they say but also understanding their emotions and perspectives. Validate them and show them that you're listening by maintaining eye contact and providing non-verbal cues like nodding. Our body language matters.

Be present in the conversation and take their feelings and criticisms seriously. Don't be distracted by external forces. Never multitask while someone is communicating with you. Listen to and reflect on what they are saying before responding. Be sure to ask open-ended questions to encourage them to share more, and remember one thing: if they are communicating it, it's important.

Use Neutral Language to Curb Defensiveness

Your choice of words can significantly impact the tone of your communication. To prevent defensiveness and promote understanding, avoid accusatory language, and instead focus on the specific behavior or issue. Accusations will lead your stepparent to focus on defending themselves rather than understanding you or your perspective. That is not a desired goal. Instead, discuss how an action or event made you feel.

Use "We" Statements

Using "we" instead of "you" statements conveys that you are in this together, working as a team to resolve a problem. Relationships are a two-way street, so what better way to show that you're trying to expand your relationship? It is important to communicate that you are practicing empathy as well as acknowledging their feelings and perspectives.

Don't Say This

"You never understand where I'm coming from." This is a generalization. They may know where you're coming from at times, and saying otherwise is a good way to halt the conversation from desired outcomes. This puts an immediate negative connotation on the conversation and also puts them into defensive mode.

Instead, Say This

"We seem to have a disconnect sometimes in our communication." Emphasizing "we" makes the conversation more about finding solutions together rather than pointing fingers, which can often lead to a more productive and less confrontational discussion.

Use "I" Statements

Expressing yourself without becoming overly aggressive can be challenging when faced with a conflict, especially if your parents are pushing your buttons or have been acting out a lot recently. To help de-escalate the situation and clarify your point, an "I" or an assertive statement is an effective psychiatrist-approved approach. Suppose there's a conflict where you feel your parents are always getting involved with your life in ways you don't necessarily want them to be involved.

Don't Say This

"You are always nagging me." Again, this is a generalization and carries a negative connotation.

Instead, Say This

"I feel a little overwhelmed when you assert your opinion or offer unsolicited advice. I would like us to set boundaries for this so we can always be on the same page."

This "I" statement expresses your feelings and needs without blaming or accusing them. After all, if you're having this conversation, it's because your stepparent wants to help—even when you don't want them to. Using language that emphasizes how *you feel* is much more effective communication and is less likely to result in them shutting down or getting angry. It also aids in their ability to empathize and see things from your perspective. Here's another example.

Don't Say This

"You never listen to me." This is also a generalization.

Instead, Say This

"I feel frustrated when I feel unheard. I would like it if we worked on listening to each other a little more effectively." This type of communication makes it so that each of you has something to work on.

After all, we all could use a little extra help in effective communication and active listening.

Speaking this way also avoids tactics of attack, critique, and criticism, which usually lead to more hostility and defensiveness. In general, using "I" messages can create a constructive dialogue about the true causes of any conflict by avoiding aggressive behaviors and fostering effective communication.

Communicate Dynamics and Expectations

It can be easy to fall into societal norms or societal expectations of what stepfamily life should look like, but these are almost never helpful. Truth is, as frustrating as it can be at times, there is no one-size-fits-all approach to family dynamics in general, and stepfamilies are certainly no exception to that. Once the new stepfamily has formed, no matter if this happened years ago, it's important to discuss what expectations are.

If your family has not done this and you feel it needs to be addressed, communicate the need to have a family discussion. This can help everyone understand what is expected in terms of family structure and what kinds of behaviors are acceptable (or not).

If you're an adult, this kind of conversation can be easier to address. If you're still an adolescent, it may take a lot more patience and care when trying to ease your family into a conversation like this. That is because emotions can run high in situations like this. At times, family counseling is the best place to address these issues.

If you're an adult and this is something your family has discussed, it may be worth re-visiting at different stages in your life, just as it is equally important to discuss your biological parents' roles in your life as you grow and transition through life.

Being in a blended family can be a positive experience for everyone if you let go of the negativity surrounding it. Stepparents can play central roles in your life, and everyone can have the opportunity to build stronger relationships by having them involved. This includes both biological parents, even if one may not be re-married. No matter the negativity surrounding this new family dynamic, everyone can get closer if proper expectations and boundaries are established.

Important note: Do not let negativity from *any* of your parents (including your stepparent) hurt any of your other relationships.

Things to discuss

- How involved will your stepparent be in decision-making as you grow and mature? Does this differ from your biological parents?

- How often should you schedule family check-ins to see what works/what doesn't?

Establish Open Communication

Effective and open communication is foundational to the success of your blended family. Your stepparent likely had a conversation with their partner (your biological parent) about how to incorporate the differences from one family to another when first getting together—at least in some facet.

Keep in mind that it can be a challenging adjustment when you marry someone with children; children that likely already have an established bond/relationship with both parents. This is not just an adjustment to your biological parents and you but for the stepparent, too. When you empathize with them, it can be easier to establish communication.

Start with these steps.

- **Agree to Talk:** Agree to talk openly with your stepparent. Be clear, concise, and honest about everything. Make sure that your discussion is private, just between the two of you, as often as possible. This will help keep the conversation on course and eliminate outward opinion or input. Remember that listening is essential to good communication.

- **Share Emotions**: Agree to support your stepparent through their varied emotions and allow them to do the same. Bottling up emotions is unhealthy and counterintuitive to open communication. Encourage your stepparent to speak freely, and agree to treat them with respect and patience. Reassure them that there's a safe space in your communication for them to be honest and open.

- **Value and Respect Every Member of the Family:** This includes your stepparent and their children (if they have them). Keep an open mind and the communication floor to all members of the family as well. This will help everyone stay connected.

Your compassion is essential in helping your blended family, as well as helping your stepparent, feel welcome and wanted. Some additional ways to effectively open the door to open communication are by setting clear boundaries.

Setting limits with children helps them to feel a sense of security; the same can be said for adults, specifically your parents or stepparents. When someone understands where a boundary line lies, they feel secure knowing that when they operate within those limits, everyone remains happy and satisfied.

Deal with Unresolved Issues from Your Biological Parents

Communicating about past issues or traumas may be necessary to continue your relationship with your parents and establish a new one (or expand upon one) with your stepparent. It is important that we do this carefully and respectfully and avoid language and situations that could flare the issue.

First thing first: acknowledge and recognize the trauma or issue for what it is.

If you had real trauma in your childhood, don't minimize the event or dismiss it by pretending it didn't happen. Don't succumb to feelings of guilt or self-blame. Acknowledge it for its true nature because that is the first and only way you begin to heal.

The next thing is to regain control. Feelings of helplessness can carry well over into adulthood and can make you feel and act like a victim, causing you to make choices based on your past. When you're a victim, you hold no control because the past is in control. If you're seeking a relationship with your parents and stepparent(s) having felt helpless or traumatized by their behavior, it is always best to seek professional help in therapy. Consider family counseling for the safety and wellbeing of all of you.

However, if you feel there are issues from your childhood that you need to discuss with your parents, and you don't feel you need professional intervention, just make sure that you're communicating with them respectfully, using neutral language, and not negating their feelings. Remember to demonstrate active listening, respect one another, and give each other space as needed.

Attend Family Counseling if Necessary

Many times, when couples are experiencing marriage again after a divorce, a new spouse isn't the only addition to the family. There are a lot of additions and transitions that need to be taken into account.

Second marriages may represent a sense of hope for your biological parent, but they may also include a season filled with challenges and transition. For newlyweds with children from previous relationships, it is especially important to manage any expectations regarding the new family dynamic. While fiction often romanticizes the lives of blended families, everyone's feelings should be brought under consideration.

Even if there are no hard feelings from the other biological parent, it is likely you (as the child) have had a few conflicting emotions from the situation. When two families are coming together as one, tensions can quickly arise. Despite everyone's determination to become the perfect blended family, it typically falls short. In fact, there are many challenges blended families struggle with and they can include the following.

Having to Cope or Sacrifice: It may be difficult when you're a child and have to undergo changes quickly, and, like most children of blended families, without a lot of warning. This can be missing out on certain opportunities you were once accustomed to or having less financial freedom than you and your family might have had before your stepparent came into the picture.

Being Inclusive: Perhaps you had new stepsiblings and even if you enjoyed time together, there might have been a sense of feeling left out on occasion—whether that be with their friends, other family members, or even with them directly. Or maybe you don't have stepsiblings but felt a difficult time feeling included or including everyone from the blended family. It is not unusual for one or more of the people in a blended family to experience feelings of isolation. This can lead to negative feelings from your stepparent or blended family. If you can't overcome that with this guide, counseling could be beneficial.

Keeping up with New Schedules: A lot of things changed when your parent and stepparent got married. If you were still a child, your parent and stepparent likely had to keep track of a ton of schedules (especially if your stepparent also had children). This included academics, sports, hobbies, etc. Establishing a routine might have been difficult, and you might have had to give up some things you held dear—which goes along with the coping and sacrificing section—and you might hold onto some resentment for that. Or maybe just schedules in general are a sore spot for you now. Whatever the case, if you feel negative about a particular issue such as this, communicate that to your parent and stepparent, even if it's been years since. Remember that your feelings are valid. The sooner you understand that, the sooner you're able to move forward and develop a stronger relationship with everyone.

Communication is key, and if you feel you struggle to communicate, consider family therapy with a therapist who specializes in blended families.

Schedule Personal Time for Reflection and Understanding

Allocating time for personal reflection and understanding enhances self-awareness and empathy. It gives proper time for each person in any given relationship to discover their unique needs as well as their strengths and weaknesses. Admitting personal faults to ourselves—let alone others—isn't easy. So, consider setting aside moments for self-reflection. Specialists also recommend you journal these thoughts to better understand your emotions and to have the ability to look back at your progress. Encourage your family members to do the same, and share your insights with one another when you're ready.

Use this personal time to explore your progress and how those advancements align with your parents' and stepparent's journey of self-awareness. Self-awareness refers to a clear understanding of your own emotions, strengths, weaknesses, thoughts, and beliefs and how they might influence your behavior, including your interactions with others. Being self-aware is fundamental for healthy relationships with yourself and others. Understanding ourselves means understanding our needs, expectations, boundaries, and communication styles. All this shapes how we interact and love our family members and friends. When we're not self-aware, we open the door to harmful interactions due to blind spots in our communication and waning emotional health. A lack of self-awareness can lead to:

- Poor emotional regulation, which results in outbursts and other unhealthy expressions of anger or hurt.

- Personal neglect and impaired mental health.

- A skewed perception of reality due to biases and defense mechanisms that build up over time. (Also, without self-awareness, a person tends to reject constructive criticism, thus missing out on potential personal growth.)

- Communication blind spots.

- Crossing boundaries, whether your own or others'.

Being more self-aware gives us the tools necessary to have satisfying and successful relationships. It just makes sense. Know yourself, and you'll have the foundation for a life and relationship that isn't just surviving but thriving.

Share Personal Growth Moments

Using feedback obtained from your scheduled meetings, emotional discussions, and self-awareness exercises, you can begin to document your personal development. Once again, journaling is a great way to record feedback and your own reflections. It can provide a glimpse of previous versions of yourself and give greater insight into your personal growth.

Personal growth is an ongoing journey. Share these moments of realization—even epiphanies—with your loved ones. Discuss your personal experiences, challenges, and lessons learned through self-reflection and check-ins with your parents. Nothing feels better than knowing we've helped someone, so when your parents help you out, be sure to tell them!

Along the way, support one another's aspirations and encourage continued self-improvement exercises. Then, go on to celebrate milestones in your personal development journey together. By following these guidelines and strategies, you can improve your communication with your stepparent, whether they are CDs or MYs, no matter where each of you are in your relationship. Effective communication is the key to understanding, empathy, and building a strong and thriving relationship.

Respect Their Space and Yours

Whether you're an adult or a child, ensure that you're giving your stepparent and yourself much-needed space. This not only helps you recoup if you're a CD, but it also gives you time to reflect on yourself. If you're an adult and your stepparent comes to visit, welcome them warmly. If you still live with them (or they live with you), show respect for their space. When you're in their rooms, try to make them feel like you are visiting their house. And likewise, ask them to respect your space as well.

Communicate where boundaries need to be and what works best for your family.

If you don't live with them, it is crucial that you communicate timeframes and expectations for visiting and going out together. Make sure you all respect your individual needs and give each other space when necessary.

Key Takeaways

Effective communication forms the foundation of all healthy and flourishing relationships. It goes beyond the confines of personality types, but learning about them can be a great place to start. This chapter has explored how you might engage with your stepparent on a deeper level and communicate about issues that you may have with them or the past you have together.

Start difficult discussions by expressing feelings without instigating conflicts. It is important, no matter what happens, to remain calm and collect yourself before delving headfirst into the conversation. Remember, others are a lot more likely to consider your perspective if they feel that they can voice their concerns without you jumping off the deep end or responding out of anger and vice versa.

Here are the best ways to express yourself without conflict.

- **Express Feelings with Words, Not Actions:** If you feel anger rising to an uncontrollable level, take a step back and return to the conversation after you've calmed down. Consider engaging in other activities that help you regain your composure. Encourage your stepparent to do the same. Use methods like walking, deep breathing, or journaling to manage strong emotions constructively.

- **Address One Issue at a Time:** Avoid resorting to the "kitchen sink" approach. Focus on one issue at a time when discussing conflicts.

- **Resist Underhandedness:** Steer clear of using underhanded or hurtful tactics when discussing sensitive topics with your parents. Attacking them in sensitive areas only fosters distrust, anger, and vulnerability, which is counterproductive to communication.

- **Be Specific and Productive:** When expressing concerns, be specific and avoid making generalized statements using words like "never" or "always." Broad complaints are challenging to address and usually aren't even true.

Once all of you can communicate effectively, make sure that you are demonstrating active listening skills during conversations and that you're using neutral language. "I" and "We" statements are best to be employed to emphasize that you are working together for a common goal and not that you are attacking them.

CDs may be a little less vocal during communications, and that's okay! Appreciate the silence. Allow them the space and time to collect their thoughts and feelings. Avoid pressuring them to speak immediately after a conflict, and create a safe environment where silence is just considered a part of the communication process.

Mys, on the other hand, don't do as well with silence. Make sure that you are offering verbal affirmations to help them feel safe and loved during communication. Compliment them genuinely.

The next thing we learned about is how the dynamic may shift as you grow older. Recognizing that the relationship you have with your stepparent evolves just as with your biological parents. The moment you begin to see them as individuals with their own lives and identities is crucial. This transition can even lead to a friendship if boundaries are respected as these transitions occur.

Remember to deal with any past or unresolved issues respectfully and check in with your parents often after important conversations or when boundaries have been set just to get an idea of how everyone is feeling and gauge how everyone feels it's going.

Make sure you schedule personal time for reflection and communicate your findings with your family during these check-ins; and finally, respect one another and the space that you all may need individually.

By following these guidelines and strategies, you can improve your communication with your stepparent, fostering understanding, empathy, and a strong, thriving relationship as you navigate the shifting dynamics of your relationship.

Chapter Three

Try to Level Emotionally

In Chapter 3 of our guide, we delve into the importance of leveling emotionally with your stepparent. This chapter explores various aspects of building and maintaining a strong emotional connection with your stepparent and highlights the value of open communication, which was explained in Chapter 2: Communication is Everything.

We explore how to overcome feeling afraid to talk about certain things with our parents and stepparents alike—which allows for the ability to truly open up and also the importance of understanding differing perspectives. We then move into other areas to improve the emotional bond you have with your stepparent in general and how you might show your appreciation for them.

Your stepparent—just as you and your biological parents are—is an emotional being, and they appreciate effort. This chapter delves into making them a priority and learning how to devote time and energy to making them happy and fostering the growth of your relationship.

Talk to Them

This means more than just casual conversations. Speaking to your stepparent is crucial. It can be about nothing at all to build and maintain a rapport, of course, but true emotional closeness happens during deep and vulnerable conversations. Talking about your problems can help reduce stress and give you much-needed catharsis or just give you a chance to vent. In fact, regular family communication can affect your psychological well-being. Communication with your family is important for your development, and it has been proven to have many benefits.

These benefits include:

- Identity formation
- Exploration of identity
- Moral reasoning
- Physical and psychological maturity

Why It Can Be Difficult to Speak to Your Stepparent

There are several reasons it may be difficult to speak to your stepparent. It could be that you have difficulty leveling with them specifically, or perhaps you struggle speaking to any of your parents.

Differing Perspectives

During adolescence, parents often don't see things the same way you do. Research reports that many teenagers feel their families are not open, cohesive, or adaptable—and overall have a slew of unaddressed problems, whereas those same reports show that their parents have differing opinions.

It is likely that you and your parents see things differently in your family, and that this issue has transcended your childhood and seeped into adulthood. What you think is lacking, your parents may be perfectly content with. This could potentially lead to a major disconnect and make communication increasingly more difficult.

Shame or Fear

Even in a situation where you feel you might have a fairly open relationship with your stepparent and can freely speak to them, it can still be potentially daunting. This is generally in regard to topics or incidents that trigger feelings of shame and embarrassment.

Talking to your stepparent about subjects such as your own (or their) mental health or even sexuality can be particularly difficult because those subjects are typically covered in stigmas from the jump. Feeling anxious about being judged, perceived negatively, or even misunderstood prevents people from opening up in general, so it is to be expected that it could be difficult to open up to your parents or any other adults (your stepparent) in these sorts of situations. You may not want anyone to think less of you or be disappointed. In such a situation, silence may seem easier than talking.

Not Feeling Close Enough

This may be an issue you have with your stepparent exclusively or all of your parents. Use this guide to grow closer to your parents and learn how to communicate and talk with them to grow a bond. If this is still a struggle, consider a family counseling session.

How to Talk to Your Stepparent

Here are some tips for talking to your stepparent.

- **Define the Intention—If There Is One:** If you need to talk to your stepparent about something in particular, especially something difficult, make sure you have that purpose laid out in your mind. Also, make sure you have a good idea of the outcome you're hoping for in the conversation. If you need them to meet a need for you, decide what that need is and have ideas set aside as to how they might meet them. Do you need them to clarify something for you? Do you need them to solve a problem? Discover exactly what you're hoping to accomplish with this conversation.

- **Prepare and Organize Your Thoughts:** Whether you want to write things down, type them out on your phone, or practice the conversation in front of the mirror, prepare yourself before having a difficult conversation. Try to organize your thoughts so that you feel more confident during the conversation. Once this is done, determine a time and a place; and if you can, tell your parents you have something important to discuss with them and ask them when a good time would be.

- **Dispel Negative Emotions:** If you need to talk to your stepparent about something that is causing you to struggle emotionally, make sure you let them know you're going to be speaking about something that is difficult for you. Even if it's something that may disappoint or upset them, making them aware of your mental state may help them set aside their negative emotions and take extra care to make it a comfortable space for you.

- **Try to Understand Their Perspective:** There will be many things that you and your parents don't agree on, and stepparents are no exception to that. This may be even—or especially—true as you get older. Generational gaps can play a big role in this. It's important to use active listening (as discussed in Chapter 2) to truly understand them and their point of view.

- **Explain If You Need Something Specific from Them:** For the conversation to go well, it is important to be clear about what you need from your stepparent if there's something specific that you need. For example, do you need their advice, or do you just want to share your feelings? Your parents will be able to respond to you better if they are aware of your needs up front. If you absolutely don't want their advice, make sure you tell them that you're just wanting to share your feelings before you even get too far into the conversation.

- **Prepare for the Worst-Case Scenario:** During a difficult conversation, it is possible that your stepparent will disagree with you. They are people with autonomy! They have a right to disagree with you! Have the conversation anyway. If you ask yourself "What's the worst that can happen after this discussion?" and you come to terms with, or accept that it may not change anything, then you will feel glad that you tried anyway.

- **Seek Professional Support:** When all else fails, you don't want to give up on your relationship. If you feel you're having difficulty talking, or some barriers are too difficult to overcome, it is important to know that there are several resources available that can help you navigate any sort of communication obstacles you may have with your parents.

What to Talk About

As covered above, conversations with your stepparent can include casual themes or involve your shared interests. You don't have to have an in-depth conversation every day, but make sure you're touching on more vulnerable topics or establishing open communication in your relationship to truly grow your bond. A great start in forming a bond that allows for vulnerability is to simply ask them about their day.

Don't Wait for Them to Take the Lead

Stepparents may wait for you to take the lead due to their status in your family dynamic. They may feel like a foreigner in your family and either be uncomfortable or just be taking psychologists' advice and waiting for you to come to them. If you feel that your stepparent is distant emotionally, and they're the type to engage with others and are quite pleasant to you in other ways, try to make the first move.

In the intricate dance of parent-child relationships, it's easy to fall into a familiar routine. It is possible your stepparent—even if you have a well-established relationship (even in a typical parent/child dynamic)—falls into the trap of routine. Perhaps they're busy, and so are you, and they don't make the move to converse, hang out, or see you as often as either of you would like.

In these sorts of situations, it's important to realize something: as adults, we hold equal responsibility for nurturing our connections, even when it's a parent/child or stepparent/child relationship/connection. Waiting for someone else to steer the ship can lead to missed opportunities for understanding, bonding, and, most importantly, reciprocal love. Initiating conversations with your stepparent (as mentioned earlier) is a fundamental step in this journey.

Don't let your relationship fall to the wayside due to routine, or even worse, pride.

As you get older, make sure that you're leveling with them on your own, without the need for them to make the first move. Ask your stepparent about their day, their interests, or their most sacred thoughts. Be as real with them as you would a friend, and have an open conversation. By showing an active interest in their lives, you create an atmosphere of engagement and openness. This not only fosters stronger communication but also deepens the emotional connection between you.

Not waiting for your stepparent to take the lead means recognizing that love and communication are reciprocal, and that communication works two ways. And if you have never established a relationship, or if they're still new to your family, it's important to recognize that they may just be giving you space.

When you actively participate in the exchange, it's a powerful demonstration of your care and appreciation for them. By initiating conversations, asking thoughtful questions, and expressing your thoughts and experiences, you're building bonds that can span a lifetime.

Offer Surprise Gestures

MY personality types tend to gravitate toward surprise gestures more than their CD counterparts, but everyone enjoys feeling special. No matter where your stepparent may fall in the personality spectrum, it is almost certain that they can appreciate a random surprise gesture!

Cook for Them

There is an old saying, "The family that eats together, stays together." Cook for your family—either lunch or dinner—and include your stepparent!

Enjoy food and time together. This is a great opportunity to bond and spend quality time with each other and forge a truly healthy dynamic.

Call Them Often

If you are living far away from your stepparent, or at least far enough that weekly visits are out of the question, make sure you call them as often as you can. Take advantage of all the good that technology can bring and make your stepparent feel as though you are still close to them even if you're actually far away. Over the call, you can even opt to FaceTime or video call, and show them what's new with you rather than just telling them! This can be a great way to be in the room with them without being in the room with them.

Go With Them on a Trip

A change of weather and location is a natural way to refresh and rejuvenate. It would also give you a chance to unwind from the monotony of life. Take a small road trip with your stepparent or invite them on a weekend getaway.

Surprise Them with Gifts

No need to wait on special occasions. Sometimes the best gifts are "just because" gifts. Pampering your stepparent is a great way to help them feel loved and appreciated. So, schedule a gift delivery to their home or take it to them yourself, and make them smile from ear to ear.

Make A Surprise Visit to Them

If your parents (and stepparent) always seem to want to spend time with you and you just haven't had a lot of time, consider making a surprise visit to them and spending the weekend. They would love it, and you could get a lot of much-needed bonding time. Spend the whole weekend with them (and if you have your own family now, take them with you), talk to them, and lend a hand whenever the opportunity calls for it!

Pamper Them with Spa Day

Just because they may not be used to it or maybe have never even had it, don't sleep on the fact that a spa day is great for rejuvenating the soul! Sometimes our parental figures forget to take care of themselves. So, book a spa appointment for them so you can help them to relax and recharge their batteries. Consider booking a couple's spa for them if they're still together so that they can spend some cozy time with one another.

Help Them With House Work

If you live with them, or nearby, the best way to pamper and surprise them is to help them with their daily or seasonal chores.

Organize Family Get-Togethers

Family get-togethers may seem daunting to some families, whether they're blended families or not! If this isn't you, then congratulations! However, if the idea of family get-togethers (or choosing between family members in your blended family) seems daunting, start with a little organization. With some creativity and planning, you can throw a stress-free family get-together. This can be anything from a family reunion to a regular ol' block party or holiday event.

If you're hoping to grow your relationship with your stepparent, then make sure you include them. This can be with both sides of your family, or just one. Remember, you're not choosing over family members. You're just planning a get-together. Responding to negativity surrounding something innocent is not necessary and can be a great deal of benefit to you if you choose to ignore negativity entirely.

When deciding on a family get-together, think about your invitees, the place and time, and specifics such as food (will this be over mealtime, or are snacks more appropriate?). After you plan all this out, you will have a much easier time planning the rest.

If there is a specific event or get-together that your biological parent and stepparent do together, consider taking this over for them for the year (or indefinitely if they're getting older and are having a difficult time continuing the tradition). It can alleviate some stress from them and give you a chance to toss your creative flair into the mix and also create new, refreshing family memories.

Remember, planning is the key to organizing a successful family get-together. Work with your parents to determine the specifics on who to invite, your time and place, and food. It may seem obvious to you who to invite, but if you have a large family, the guest list could become overwhelming, especially if you aren't used to hosting. Also, make sure you get their input and expertise on a few traditions to what you should refresh and what you should keep the same.

Hosting a family get-together is hard work, but it can give you and your parents an amazing bonding experience as well.

Include Them

Do you feel like you belong when you're in your friend group? Or what about at work? Have you ever felt like you didn't belong? How would you feel if it was your family unit where you felt you didn't belong?

Being truly inclusive is ensuring everyone is invited to that barbeque or that everyone participates in the family Christmas name drawing. Being included is where that sense of belonging comes in that allows people to feel safe and valued. Human beings are wired with a primal need to feel as though they belong and like they're part of a pack or a group. Research has shown that when individuals lack a sense of belonging, they feel threatened and spend energy in masking or pretending that they are something they're not. This leads to diminishing mental health and the thought-process that we aren't worthy of others' time. Who would want someone to feel that way? Certainly not you! Not if you're reading this guide! Chances are if you're reading this, you want others to feel psychologically safe and nurtured if they're spending time with you. After all, feeling psychologically safe allows you to open up and have a willingness to understand others' opinions and thought processes without quickly judging or jumping to conclusions.

Respect and Kindness Go a Long Way

Treat your stepparent with respect and kindness. Of course, just because you are trying to include them in your life and make them feel worthy and included in general doesn't mean you have to include them on everything. It's important to have your own space, and it's also necessary to have your own boundaries.

How can you help them feel more included?

Ask Them: The first way you can help your stepparent feel more included is to ask them what they might want to be included in or if they feel included in your everyday life. If they have feedback, make sure you're listening to it (using your active listening skills), that you take what they say seriously, and remember not to be defensive if it's not the feedback you want to hear. Sometimes we don't realize how others perceive what we're doing until we ask them. Recognize that your stepparent may have feedback for you that might have been difficult for them to communicate to you, and you should be grateful that they took the opportunity to do so. This will only strengthen your relationship in the long run.

Build a Better Connection: By using this guide, you're already well on your way to doing this, but another best practice in learning how to include someone is by building a better connection to them so you can understand where they might be coming from or how you might include them. Getting to know their passions and interests can help you come up with things to engage them and keep them feeling included. Likewise, by including them more often, you're also building a better connection with them. So, the two ideals feed off each other continually.

Keep Them Involved: If you usually go to your parents about certain things, ask yourself if there's a reason your stepparent can't also be included in these situations. If you go to your parents for advice on something, consider asking your stepparent for their advice, too. In addition, if you run to your parents during certain times of sadness or disappointment, consider reaching out to your stepparent too. This could be just the sort of inclusion that they are craving from you.

Write Them Letters

Although talking to your stepparent about what you are thinking or feeling can be a challenge, it is possible to try to communicate something emotional for you by letter instead. This can take pressure off by allowing you the outlet you need to get things off your chest and allowing them to receive the information in a private space where they can properly process their feelings. Remember, although you can do this to express your feelings on big subject matters you don't want to discuss in person, you can also use this as a way to grow closer emotionally and the occasion can be "just because."

Regardless of the subject matter, before beginning make sure you:

- Starting a book club with them.
- Stretching it out with some yoga, whether at a studio or home.
- Playing games or doing a puzzle together.
- Gardening together.
- Staring a collection.
- Beer brewing at home.
- Learning how to knit together.

Activities you may want to try with your MY stepparent include:

- Trying your hand at tie-dying.
- Learning a new language together.
- Cooking together.
- Going to an unknown band's concert.
- Trying a martial arts class.
- Going camping or biking.
- Rock climbing.
- Volunteering at a local soup kitchen.

Offer to Help Them

Let's face it, no one is getting any younger. It's important to show your stepparent that you're appreciative of them, just as you would your biological parents, and that you care enough to want to help them.

Around the House

Does it seem that even though you are out of the house your stepparent still seems super busy? They may be still working hard running the home you grew up in and even maintaining their job, whether it be with just the two of them (your biological parent and stepparent) or if you have younger siblings still in the house.

You can show them how much you appreciate them by helping out with chores around the house when you have extra time on your hands (or even better, prioritize the time to help them). Ask them what you can do to help them if you're not sure where you might be most needed. They will likely appreciate your thoughtfulness!

If your family has a dog, a cat, a bird, a fish, or any animal that eats—or if they got it after you left the nest—offer to help take care of them when you're hanging out around the house or visiting. You could also be a huge help and take them out for a walk, play fetch, or play with them with other toys.

More chores around the house you can do include:

- Let go of any past resentments.
- Develop realistic expectations.
- Cherish the good.

Let Go of Past Resentments

Having ongoing resentments toward a parent or a stepparent does more than just keep them in the doghouse. In fact, it keeps us from truly feeling free, too. We forever have a victim mentality, and clinging to issues from our past is a way of keeping them with you forever.

No matter if you're upset with your stepparent for "breaking up" your biological family (which generally is not the case) or for something else that happened in childhood, it's important to recognize that you need to resolve those resentments and move forward. This is true whether you want a relationship going forward or not.

Develop Realistic Expectations

If there are unresolved issues of your past that you need to forgive, make sure you're setting realistic expectations not only for your stepparent, but for yourself, your healing, and the relationship itself. If there were a lot of toxic issues in your childhood, having a close and healthy functioning relationship may not be practical without a lot of family counseling. Consider this when setting your expectations. On the flip side, though, if you don't have a lot of personal resentments, make sure that you're not setting the bar too low, especially if you want a relationship with your stepparent.

The sins of our stepparents (just as with parents) may be the hardest to forgive. This is especially true if your stepparent came into your life when you were young enough to bond with them maternally or paternally just as you would a biological parent. This is because we—as children—often view our parents through rose-colored lenses. We expect the world out of them and have high expectations that we refuse to lower. Recognizing that they are human is a great first step in developing realistic expectations and forgiving them!

Cherish the Good

Most parents love their children. There are, of course, exceptions, but where does that leave our stepparents? It is important to know that not everyone's experience is the same in this. Some stepparents do unequivocally love their stepchildren. Some, however, do not; and some do, but like biological parents, have no idea how to show it.

The truth is that no parent is perfect—which means that everyone has wounds from their childhood to a degree. However, there are good times. Cherish those. Think about good things your stepparent has done for you, and hold on to them. Avoid forgetting the negative and instead talk it out and communicate your displeasure to work through it, but do remember to cherish the good times.

Key Takeaways

Chapter 3: Try to Level Emotionally underscores the significance of developing and maintaining an emotional connection with your stepparent. Using these suggestions with the open communication theme explored in Chapter 2, you can truly navigate the complexities of not only establishing but nurturing your emotional bond with your stepparent.

Talk to your parents and overcome communication barriers. Overcoming obstacles in communication is crucial. Acknowledge that differing perspectives, fear, and feelings of inadequacy might hinder open dialogue. Overcome these by:

- Surprising them with small gestures of affection.

- Sharing experiences.
- Exploring mutual hobbies.
- Including them in family functions.
- Writing them letters.
- Volunteering together.
- Helping them, whether that be financially, domestically, or just by lending an ear.

No matter what you choose to implement in your relationship with your stepparent, remember that a meaningful emotional connection demands proactive engagement and sincere effort. Prioritizing communication, consistent support, and active participation in shared activities lays the foundation for enduring emotional bonds, enriching the family dynamic and nurturing mutual growth and understanding. Make sure that you're consistent and have the best intentions in mind to truly develop this relationship!

Chapter Four

Celebrate the Dynamic

Life is made up of moments—some good, some bad, but all significant in shaping who we are as people. As adults, your relationships continue to evolve, and you often find yourself craving deeper connections. If you're reading this, that deeper connection you crave is with your stepparent. One powerful way to nurture this sort of deep connection is by merely celebrating good times together.

In this chapter, we'll explore the idea of inviting your stepparent over for dinner, letting them contribute where they can, and creating new traditions together.

This chapter will guide you on not only celebrating with your stepparent but also how to navigate the shifting dynamic and celebrating the differences as you age. You used to celebrate holidays with your parents because they threw the parties or your teacher had you make them a Mother's Day or Father's Day gift, but now that you're an adult, you have a choice about how to celebrate—and who to celebrate. Using this guide, you can create a balance in a way that makes everyone happy and helps your stepparent feel like just as much of a priority as anyone else.

Invite Them Over for Dinner

Your parent and stepparent have to eat. Invite them both over for dinner at your place—whether it's just you or you have a family. This is a great opportunity to let them into your world as an adult.

Let Them Bring Something

If they ask what to bring, don't tell them "nothing." Have them bring something! Ask them to bring an appetizer or even a family-favorite dessert (your family, or even something that is a tradition in their family before they married your biological parent) if they are up to it. Contributing to the meal might make them feel special, and if they bring something that resonates positively with them and their traditions, it may make it even more special. However, if they're a bit older and have difficulty in the kitchen, maybe ask if they could bring a bottle of wine or a beverage.

Get Them a Ride

Sometimes as your parents age, it's difficult to get them to visit. Your stepparent is no exception unless they're significantly younger than your biological parent. However, generally speaking, your parent and stepparent are both getting older—and maybe this contributes to them not visiting as much as you would like. This could be due to a multitude of factors, but for many, the older our parents and stepparents get, the less likely they are comfortable driving far or at night. Advanced services such as Uber or Lyft (or even a run-of-the-mill taxi company) can make the task a lot more simple. You and/or your partner no longer have to worry about them getting to you—which can mean more time to prepare your meal!

Choose a Meal That is Tasty but Recognizable

Ask your stepparent if there's something they might want or what they would like to bring. If they want to bring a specific side dish, think of a meal that might go well with that dish. The goal is to be accommodating to them, their traditions, and their tastes as well as implement some of your—and your family's—favorite traditions or dishes. This is all about inclusion and cohesiveness. You want to fuse as much of each other's traditions together as possible. You never know, you may end up finding a new favorite meal.

Keep in mind that older generations also have their favorite dishes and are generally less flexible, so beware of deviating too much from that. If you're looking for a healthy dish, choose one of your parents' favorites but substitute a couple of healthy ingredients. For example, consider ground turkey instead of ground beef or Greek yogurt for cream. These small swaps won't jeopardize the taste to pickier parents who may be used to the original dishes and can also be what you and your family need for your appetites.

Celebrate Your Parent and Stepparent's Anniversary

This may be difficult, especially if you don't feel you have a good relationship yet with your stepparent or if it's a new dynamic. This may feel like a betrayal to your biological parent or the relationship that your parents shared. But one of the best ways to include your stepparent and help them feel like they belong and are valuable to you is to show them that you value their happiness and the happiness of the biological parent they're married to.

Celebrating their union is an excellent way to do this, and if you feel yourself struggling to accept and celebrate this, ask yourself if you're ready to celebrate the new family dynamic. If you aren't, there is no shame in voicing what is holding you back—or seeking counseling if you feel that is something you may need.

Remember, you don't have to forget about your biological parents' anniversary. In fact, it's completely healthy to recognize that day because it is essentially the day that led to your existence and the family dynamic you knew before. However, don't expect your biological parents to celebrate that day anymore, and don't feel the need to be vocal about the day. It may not be healthy for them or their future relationships.

Remember, your biological parents' failed relationship is not your stepparent's fault, and it isn't yours either. You don't have to participate in breathing negative energy into the relationship they have, even if it's difficult for you to accept emotionally. You also don't have to let anyone else make you feel guilty for trying to accept your stepparent and the reality of your family dynamic as it is rather than how it used to be.

Create Memory Gifts

Memory gifts are a great, personalized option that is sure to make your stepparent feel good, and are a great way to memorialize good times with them. If you haven't established a lot of memories with them yet, then make sure you're making new ones and think about doing some of these as they happen!

Types of Memory Gifts:

- Personalized photo albums
- Lockets with photographs inside
- Picture ornaments

These sorts of memory gifts are amazing when you want to:

- Feel connected to loved ones.

- Have a story piece to remember your loved ones.

- Preserve your memories.

- Keep a memoir of the past to pass on to future generations.

Celebrate Them "Just Because"

In this guide, we discuss gestures and surprises for your stepparent. It is important to note that sometimes "just because" celebrations are some of the most heartfelt.

You don't need a holiday or a special occasion to send your mother flowers or ask your dad to go fishing. You just need it to be "because." This is no different for your stepparent. Consider your stepparent's individual needs, desires, or things they just enjoy doing, and try to cater to that. Take them out, keep them in, it doesn't matter. What matters is doing something special for each of them individually in a way that they will appreciate uniquely—away from your biological parent.

Thank Them for Doing Their Best

At the end of the day, your stepparent—whether they have formed into a traditional parent over the years or is someone who has established a very neutral stance in your life—is not your biological parent. In the relationship with your natural parent, they have likely had to navigate a whirlwind of emotions, issues, and situations that they did not anticipate nor envision for themselves. Regardless of what has occurred, a great way to celebrate the dynamic of your now-family is to thank your stepparent for whatever role they have had in your life and for doing their best.

In fact, remember to thank them if they provided any of the following:

- A childhood—even if it wasn't as good as you may have wanted
- Attention—even if it wasn't as much as you felt you needed
- Love—even if it wasn't as much or shown in the way that you felt you needed often (Remember, our parents show us the only the way they know, and the same can be said for our stepparents)
- Financial support—whether they struggled or didn't
- Guidance—whether you feel it was good guidance or not

Remember Them on Father's Day and Mother's Day

This can be a difficult thing, especially if your stepparent is new in your life. This doesn't have to be grand or extravagant, and it also doesn't have to be immediate. You can give yourself time and space to come up with what works best for you and your family. The truth is, stepfamilies often look entirely different from the next. Everyone's experience is different. Do what works best for your family.

Differences in Family Dynamics

Primary Parent Re-Married: In the United States, most children of divorced parents live with one parent more often than the other. In this scenario, it is very likely that if your primary parent is remarried, you have more interaction with their spouse than you would if your non-primary parent were married.

In this sort of dynamic, there are two scenarios:

- Your non-primary parent is involved.
- Your non-primary parent is rarely involved or not involved at all.

If your non-primary parent is involved, it is likely that you see your stepparent as more of a bonus parent. If that is the case, discuss with them—and your parents—how you might celebrate them on these special occasions. You don't want to cross boundaries or step on toes, but it is important to celebrate them in one way or another to make them feel valued in your family. If this isn't something that has been established, or you feel you want to change how it is established, consider doing this again as you age and go through different transitions and stages with your own life.

If your non-primary parent is rarely or not involved at all, you likely see your stepparent as a primary parent. If this is the case, discuss with them how you might celebrate your stepparent (if this hasn't already been established in the past).

Non-Primary Parent Re-Married: If your primary parent isn't remarried or you're just looking at expanding your relationship with your non-primary parent's spouse, then you may be using this guide to help. These types of relationships are generally the most difficult to grow a bond in, mostly because you spend less time with your stepparent than if they lived with you. In this sort of scenario, it may be a little easier—and less pressure—to send a text message, a letter, or a card that you're keeping them in your thoughts. However, don't be shy or feel shame or guilt if you want to kick this up a notch and do something in person. Discuss options with your family and do what is best for you.

Recognize Their Achievements and Yours—Together

Life is a journey filled with accomplishments and milestones. Celebrate your stepparent's achievements the same as you would your parents, and also celebrate with them when you reach your own.

You can do this by celebrating them in helping you achieve your goals, such as being a support to you when you graduated college, or it can be their own accomplishments. Celebrate that promotion they just got; celebrate their retirement; celebrate that big purchase they just made. Whatever achievement they have, recognize it, and celebrate them. And continue to grow your relationship by letting them know when you meet your successes and goals so they can celebrate with you!

Let them know when you're doing well so they aren't only there for you in the tough times, but also the good! Let them flood you with love. Doing these things together is a powerful way to celebrate life in general—but also celebrating your them, and the good times you have together as a family *and* individually.

Share Life-Altering Moments with Them (Even the Bad Ones)

It's easy to share good news. That new promotion, that big car or home purchase, the engagement—these are all exciting and easy to share! But make sure you're being real with your stepparents (and parents). Tell them when that break up happens, when you lose your job, when you're having trouble paying bills and you think something financially detrimental may happen.

Sharing your life moments with your family brings you closer together. Not only can they offer their advice to you, but they can also be a shoulder to lean on in times of distress. Being vulnerable with others truly allows for bonds to develop and become richer. It also allows for moments of celebration to become heightened when good times come back around.

Tell Them You Love Them

Again, not all families are the same. It's possible this guide is just being used as an extra boost to show your stepparent that you love them. Maybe you feel guilty for loving them, or you just feel you want to grow your relationship with them the same way you might your biological parent. It's also possible that you're using this guide to learn how or if you *can* love your stepparent.

Whatever the case, don't tell someone you love them if you don't. But if you feel you do, express that. Don't let worry or guilt take that away from you. If you love your stepparent, it's likely because they have done a lot for you, and they deserve to be recognized for that.

As human beings, we have an innate pull to our biological parents. It's easier to love them than our stepparents in many cases (unless your stepparent is the only parent you've ever known). If you feel yourself gravitating toward your stepparent and loving them, then there is likely a reason. Don't jeopardize your closeness or your relationship by not telling them how you feel for them.

Create Traditions

You and your family likely have your own traditions. It is also possible that your stepparent may not be completely ingrained in those traditions. If they aren't, consider allowing them to bring over their own traditions and fuse them with yours to create a more harmonious and cohesive family unit.

You can also completely start from scratch and develop your own traditions. Just make sure that you're being open and accommodating, and that all of you are consistent in making these traditions true to your family.

Key Takeaways

In Chapter 4: Celebrate the Dynamic, the focus lies on celebrating the evolving relationships with stepparents and your family dynamic with them. It also acknowledges the significance of shared moments in shaping those familial bonds. The chapter advocates inviting stepparents over for dinner, encouraging their contribution to the meal (and any traditions they may want to contribute), and facilitating their visits through thoughtful arrangements (whether that be by picking them up or sending an Uber or a Lyft).

More ways to celebrate your stepparents include:

- Commemorating special occasions, such as anniversaries.

- Creating personalized memory gifts.

- Expressing gratitude and recognizing achievements—together.

These all create a new level of closeness by validating the importance of them in your life. Furthermore, it's important when celebrating your stepparent that you remember to embrace new traditions or blend existing ones so that your stepparent can feel like a true cohesive part of the family.

Chapter Five

Appreciate Them for Who They Are

In this chapter, we delve into the essential elements of fostering a deeper and more meaningful connection with your stepparent by merely appreciating them for who they are. As adults, we often focus on building independent lives and possibly blaming our parents (and our stepparents by default at times) for certain things we feel we lack. However, appreciating them for who they are is fundamental in growing closer to them, and this includes our stepparents.

To truly appreciate your stepparent for who they are, you must realize that they are human. In this section, we delve into the reality that despite our childish thoughts when we were kids, our parents aren't superheroes, and neither are our stepparents. They're all only human. Get to know them for who they are by asking them questions to truly understand them. This chapter will help you be open and receptive to truly getting to know them and teach you how you might forgive and move forward from issues you might have from your childhood.

Celebrate Their Emotional Strengths

Celebrating the emotional strengths each person brings to the familial table is essential for bonding and growth. To love your stepparent more effectively, resonate with them emotionally.

Take the time to identify and acknowledge the unique emotional strengths each of you has. CDs often bring introspection, empathy, and stability, while MYs may contribute enthusiasm, spontaneity, and optimism. Recognize how your emotional strengths complement your stepparent's and vice versa.

CDs can provide a stabilizing presence during challenging times, while MYs can infuse energy and positivity into the mix where negativity could normally take over. are part of people's identities, and your parents have them just like everyone else.

Your stepparent having different emotional strengths than you is quite a good thing because oftentimes the relationship becomes more stable over time as a result. This is because each of you can feed off of the other's energy. Where one person lacks, the others can cover the bill and vice versa.

Express Gratitude

Regularly express your gratitude for your stepparent and the emotional strengths they bring to the table. If you've had a particularly bad day and your MY stepparent has supported you and breathed a fresh, upbeat, and optimistic breath of fresh air into your lungs, make sure you acknowledge that and express your gratitude to them. Perhaps you feel like your life is rolling down a tumultuous road, and they bring stability where you don't feel it anywhere else, even with your biological parents. Let them know how their qualities have positively impacted you. A simple "thank you" can go a long way.

Get to Know Their Personality Types and Love Languages

The 5 Love Languages, by Dr. Gary Chapman, was written in 1995 and has become incredibly popular in Western culture. The book sparked a new way of thinking about how we love and how we like to receive love. Everyone has their own "love language," and the book explains how to show someone that love in a way that they can truly hear it.

Chapman identified five love languages.

Words of Affirmation: If your stepparent is an MY, they're more likely to have this as their love language than a CD. We have all heard that "actions speak louder than words," and while this may be true, words can mean just as much as actions for certain people. Positive affirmations are incredibly important, for example, for children during the rearing ages. In fact, positive affirmations have been shown to increase mental well-being in the same way as nutrition, sleep, and exercise.

Your words of affirmation can give an MY who speaks this love language the ability to focus on the positive even in a particularly negative situation. Speak positively to your stepparent if you feel this is their love language.

Quality Time: One could argue that most people enjoy quality time in one way or another. This can be taking your stepparent on a family vacation or to a Sunday brunch for a one-on-one meal and conversation time. This could mean watching a movie with a CD or a big event for an MY. No matter what you do, just make sure you're actively participating and giving them your undivided attention.

Giving Gifts: MY and CDs both love gifts. MYs, however, may like more extravagant and bold gifts than their CD counterpart. We especially love these on special occasions. The gift can be anything; what matters is that it is given with thought behind it. You don't need to spend a lot or even anything at all. Just make sure it's special and has thought and emotion behind it!

Physical Touch: While this may be a little more difficult with your stepparent depending on your current relationship, consider if this may be your stepparent's love language. If you give everyone in your family a hug and skip your stepparent and it's their love language, this might make them feel rejected or unloved. Find out if that's the case with your stepparent, and work through your own emotions as to how you might feel about showing them physical affection. Don't make yourself uncomfortable for the sake of someone else—but don't ignore that this could be something missing from your relationship.

Acts of Service: The final love language is "acts of service," which is basically just love in action. That old saying "actions speak louder than words" rings 100% true in this scenario if that's your stepparent's love language. This can include driving them somewhere, picking up their dry cleaning, helping them around the house, etc.

No matter what love language your stepparent gravitates towards, learn it, and see what you can do to show them that you truly do love and appreciate them for who they are!

Show Interest in Their Past Before They Became a Stepparent

It's easy to see your stepparent and forget that they had an entire life before you and your biological parent (and possibly your siblings) came into the picture. We get so caught up in the day-to-day noise of life—the transactional updates and small talk or the habitual avoidance of controversial topics—that we sometimes fail to get to know our loved ones on a deeper level. If you are looking to get to know your stepparent in a whole new light, strengthen or reset your relationship, or maybe just connect your children to them, having some insight into their past may be a great place to start!

Playing the "20 Questions" game might be a great way to get to know them—and them you! It is a great, easy, and fun game to play to open the door to discovering people for who they are.

Play it at the next family gathering so that friends and family can all participate. You'll be amazed at the new light through which you will all see each other.

20 Questions to Ask Your Stepparent

- What were your favorite toys as a child?
- What was your favorite lunch when you were in school?
- What's the first major news story you remember?
- Did you have a secret fort or a tree house?
- What was your favorite room in the house you grew up in?
- What's a song that you most associate with your teenage years?
- What did you want to be when you grew up?
- What was your favorite activity as a young adult?

- What was the best thing about your wedding day to my mom/dad?
- What are the most important lessons you have learned from life?
- How are you different from your parents?
- How did you feel about becoming a stepparent?
- What was your biggest fear about becoming a stepparent?
- What is the funniest story you have about being a parent?
- What's one of the prouder moments you remember as a parent?
- What's one of the most memorable gifts you've ever received?
- What is something that you learned after it was too late?
- What's the hardest choice you've ever had to make, and who helped you make it?
- What first exposure to a breakthrough technology will you never forget?
- What is your favorite thing to do in your spare time now?

Show Gratitude for the Relationship You Have with Them

It's important that all of our loved ones feel valued and appreciated. Take time to show gratitude for your stepparent and for the relationship you currently have with them. It's best to meet people where they are, and you can always improve upon the relationship even more and show gratitude for that as it develops and strengthens as well!

Find a Good Time to Talk: If you want to let your stepparent know how much you care, find a good time to talk to them about it. People are busy, and the last thing you want to do is try to talk to them when they can't fully listen to what you're saying. This will create a divide, which would be completely counterintuitive to what you had originally sought to do.

If you know your stepparent is usually busy on a certain night of the week, don't try to talk to them on that night. This may also be true of a certain type of day. Wait until they have some downtime and talk to them then! That way they can pay attention and not have any distractions afoot.

Think About What You're Going to Say: Showing appreciation can be difficult, especially if you're not the type to discuss your emotions outwardly. You may not know exactly what to say or how to say it. It may even be possible that you need time to develop a list of things you're appreciative of. Parents do a lot for us, even our stepparents at times (and sometimes especially our stepparents) so it can be stressful to find the words that truly thank them for what they've done for you. Consider rehearsing beforehand if you're especially worked up or nervous about the conversation. Remember, this person loves you—don't be afraid to be yourself. They'll be happy to hear that you appreciate them. Don't put too much pressure on yourself to deliver an amazing speech.

Use Specifics: It can be nice to give a general "thank you," but you may also find it is quite beneficial to include some specifics when expressing gratitude to your stepparent. It will help them not only understand what is most valuable to you but that you also acknowledge what they did for you specifically. It's easy to generalize. It takes a lot more focus and time to acknowledge something specific.

Become Their Friend

Friends are important, no matter what stage of life you're in. Friends help us when we are in need, they make us feel supported, and they make things much more enjoyable. When finding a friend, what you generally do is gravitate towards people who have similar interests or hobbies as you. This is no different in making your stepparent your friend.

Be Someone Who Supports Them: Supporting someone isn't exactly rocket science but is at times difficult. It requires basic empathy and communication skills. The first step is to just listen. Giving your stepparent space to talk and listening to how they feel may be all they need. Be sure to also take the next steps necessary to reassure them, and while they're talking to you, make sure that you're patient. Above all else, avoid making assumptions when they're confiding in you.

Be Someone Who Helps Them When They're in Need: Did their tire go flat? Did they lock themselves out of the house? Did their electricity malfunction or a pipe burst? Be the person that helps them when they need help. If you have the skillset to fix the issue, do it yourself—but if you don't have the skillset, help them by suggesting someone who does or making that call yourself.

Make Things More Enjoyable: Don't be a Negative Nelly. Even though stepfamilies have their issues (as does every other family unit) you don't have to focus on the negative. Instead, be enjoyable to be around and avoid complaining all the time. If you have issues with your life or your family unit, make sure you're communicating those in a healthy and helpful way.

Have Common Interests with Them: This goes without saying, but people enjoy doing things with people who enjoy the same things as them. When you're working on growing more emotionally close with your stepparent, consider participating in those mutual hobbies that were discussed. Whether that is something your steppparent already liked or a new hobby or activity you both decided to pick up together, enjoying an activity that they also enjoy can help you appreciate your stepparent for who they are.

Key Takeaways

In Chapter 5: Appreciate Them for Who They Are, we learn to promote a deeper connection with your stepparent by appreciating them for their individuality. The chapter underlines the significance of acknowledging the humanity in both parents and stepparents, urging readers to explore their stepparent's personality, emotional strengths, and unique attributes—as well as who they were before joining your family (to do this in a fun manner, consider playing a game of "20 Questions").

Great ways to appreciate your stepparent include:

- Celebrating their emotional strengths.
- Identifying their love language and how to show them your appreciation effectively.
- Expressing gratitude for them.

Above all else, be a friend to your stepparent by being someone who offers support, has common interests, and is a joy to be around. If you do that, the relationship will grow stronger and be a lot easier to maintain in the future.

Chapter Six

Boundaries and Opinions

In this chapter, we delve into the importance of setting boundaries. Whether you cohabitate with your stepparent or not, it's crucial to establish clear boundaries and engage in open discussions about expectations. This doesn't matter if you've moved in with them or they have moved in with you. This guide will teach you how to properly set boundaries with them in your adulthood.

Communication and respect for each other's boundaries are crucial for maintaining a peaceful coexistence. This guide will also discuss taking your stepparent's advice, as it is likely still quite valuable to you, and teach you that it is equally important to listen and respect their input after they have given it. Don't hesitate to ask for help when needed, and communicate your feelings honestly. When misunderstandings occur, give your stepparent the benefit of the doubt, recognizing the limitations that they may have. To maintain mutual respect, avoid using offensive language. Lastly, this guide will teach you how to set boundaries that prioritize "you" time for self-care and personal growth and engage in activities that recharge and rejuvenate you.

Set Boundaries

Setting boundaries with your parents and stepparents alike is important for various reasons. First of all, it prevents you—or them—from building up resentment and promotes healthy and pleasant interactions.

If your stepparent is someone who has been in your life for a long time, then it's possible that when you first hit adulthood, you'll need to establish the same sort of boundaries with them, as you would your biological parents, so you can further establish individualization and learn to develop a life outside of that with your parental figures.

Without proper boundaries in place, your parent and stepparent may feel that they can impose their beliefs and opinions on you at any time they desire. And although their input can be helpful at times, it's important to establish ground rules before that advice is given.

These sorts of conversations can be difficult to have, but they are necessary in fostering a healthy relationship.

What Healthy Boundaries Look Like

Healthy boundaries with parents and stepparents alike involve mutual acknowledgment that you are an adult with your own thoughts, opinions, beliefs, experiences, and needs. You are your own human being; your own person. And as such, you have your own autonomy. Your thoughts are not theirs; your actions shouldn't be either.

This may be difficult to establish in the beginning, but they must be set so that you know how to own your needs and be able to say yes and no when you want to.

Examples of boundaries you might want to consider include:

- How frequently they visit or stop in.
- When they're allowed to have input on your relationships.
- When they should have input on raising your children.
- Is it appropriate for them to buy you things without you asking for it?
- Are they allowed to comment on your body or your personal life?

Steps to Setting Boundaries With Your Stepparent

- Learn what your unique values are, especially the ones that differ from theirs.
- Identify what you need to be consistent with your values and beliefs.
- Communicate those needs with your stepparent and be clear about what you need.
- Establish rules and guidelines to follow that will make you feel comfortable.

When You Ask Them for Advice, Respect It

While you can set boundaries for your parents and stepparents and vice versa, it's important to note the importance of respecting one another's advice during your boundary discussion. For example, if you're going to ask your stepparent for advice, don't ignore them when they give it to you. That would show that you don't respect them or their time. Going to them for advice may seem like second nature at this point, but it shouldn't be taken for granted. Or, on the flip side, if it's hard for you to ask their advice, why would you put yourself through a difficult situation not to listen to or take the advice seriously? Either way, your stepparent will feel important and trusted if you go to them for advice every once in a while. When they give you that advice, make sure you're taking proper care to heed it—or at the very least, thank them for it if you take a different route.

Know That There's Nothing Wrong with Asking for Help: As much as your pride can tell you that it's terrible to ask for help, it's not. Everyone needs it now and then, just like everyone needs advice. Remember, those who are successful in life are not those who don't have obstacles, but the ones who can find the resources and tools to make those obstacles disappear.

When You Need Help, Be the One to Bring It Up: Pick a low-key moment. Don't make it out to be some big, dramatic thing. It's always easier to talk to someone when everyone feels comfortable and relaxed.

Explain How You're Feeling: If you're having an issue with something, let your stepparent know what you're feeling and describe what you're having trouble with and how it is affecting you. If you don't quite know how to communicate it, then tell them, "I'm not sure what I'm feeling, but I don't feel like myself."

Maybe even let them know certain symptoms you have and in what way you don't feel like yourself. Maybe you're tired lately; maybe irritable. Or maybe you know exactly what's wrong. Whatever the case, communicate what you can so that they can better help you.

Say You Want Help or Advice: Don't get caught up trying to analyze or explain the whys, especially when you don't know. Let your stepparent know you need help and to what extent you feel you need it. Everyone gets nervous or upset sometimes, but let them know if it is more serious than that. They can't read your mind. At the end of the day, if you want to develop and grow your relationship with your stepparent, it's likely that you care for them and that they care for you. If you do care for them, you have to learn to trust them. Let them know you need help and let them help you decide what sort of help you need.

If You Need to, Try Again Later: Sometimes we can't bring ourselves to tell someone what is wrong. And sometimes when we're ready to talk, who we want to talk to isn't available. And sometimes, frankly, it's just not a good time. If that's the case, don't fret. It's entirely possible that your stepparents just don't have the time at the moment.

If you feel as though your stepparent is brushing you off, try again later. Sometimes people just need a little time to understand where you're coming from. If it's necessary, ask them when they may be free to talk, or confront them (respectfully) and ask why they're dodging you.

Give Them the Benefit of the Doubt During Misunderstandings

People are typically doing the best they can. Generally speaking, it's safe to assume that if a person could do better at any point, they would. As adults, we sometimes have difficulty regulating our emotions. These "adult temper tantrums" are when an adult becomes completely ungrounded and sometimes lashes out.

If those people had the necessary tools in place, don't you think they would do better?

Giving people the benefit of the doubt is all about trust, and we need to trust our stepparent, especially if we want to develop a relationship with them. You must trust that if they've done or said something that seemed out of sorts, it was due to an external factor that they couldn't quite control in that moment. Discuss how a situation made you feel, forgive them, and move on.

Remember these important truths:

- Just because you have certain tools or resources in place doesn't mean others do.
- Your life and your actions are not their lives and their actions.

It is important that we understand that none of our parents had the same upbringing as we did. They may not be equipped in the same way that we are. Always give them the benefit of the doubt, knowing that if they could have done better in any given situation, they likely would have.

Avoid Being Offensive with Your Language

Use bad language sparingly around your parents, and this includes your stepparents. Using foul language around them, even as an adult, could be seen as disrespectful and can have several implications.

It's essential to recognize that your stepparent may have played a significant role in shaping your values and behaviors. Using offensive language can be perceived as a disregard for the values they instilled in you during your childhood. Maintaining a level of respect in your interactions with them can be seen as a sign of appreciation for the guidance they've provided throughout your upbringing.

Even if your stepparent wasn't there during your younger childhood years, you don't want to make them uncomfortable, either, and even though you aren't a little kid, you are still considered their stepchild (or child). Stepparents, just like parents, might feel uncomfortable, hurt, or disrespected when they hear their child use offensive or derogatory words.

It can create a barrier to open and honest communication, making it challenging to discuss important matters or express genuine emotions.

By refraining from foul language, you help create a more conducive environment for meaningful conversations and ensure that your relationship remains built on mutual respect. Remember, as adults, you can express yourself effectively without resorting to offensive language, no matter how colorful it is and how habitual it has become in other areas of your life.

Define Relationships with All Parental Figures

When you were a child, you likely didn't have a lot of say in this. Now that you're older—possibly an older adolescent or an adult—it can be easier to define and establish clear boundaries and relationships with all of your parental figures. Perhaps you do see your stepparent as a mother or father figure. If you do, let them—and the other parents in the mix—know that is how you see them and continue your relationship based on that.

However, if you want your stepparent to take a back seat in certain situations, it's also important that you communicate that with them and your parent. Do this in a respectful way, as this can be a tender subject. It's important that you communicate your wants and needs in this situation to further strengthen your familial bond. Your family can't know that they're upsetting you or damaging the relationship if they don't know where boundaries are.

Key Takeaways

Chapter 6: Boundaries and Opinions underscores the critical aspect of establishing boundaries and embracing opinions within the stepparent-stepchild relationship. This chapter focuses on the human need for clear boundaries. Even as children, we thrive on boundaries, and all relationships should consist of boundaries because they help us feel secure in our relationships.

In this chapter, we focus on the fact that human beings rely on clearly defined boundaries to know whether they've upset someone. If those boundaries are never communicated, the likelihood that misunderstandings and inadvertent crossing of unknown boundaries rear their heads.

Boundaries are crucial in all aspects, regardless of living arrangements or age. If you're an adult, these boundaries may be a little easier to discuss (but they still may be difficult). It's important to:

- **Advocate for Open Discussions and Expectations:** By encouraging respectful communication and recognizing each other's boundaries as adults, you can maintain homeostasis in your relationship.

- **Understand Your Limits:** Release all guilt associated with boundaries and learn to respect your individual space. This is a crucial component of all healthy relationships and is also true for parent and stepparent boundaries.

- **Be Consistent:** Even though you establish boundaries, it might be easy to kick things under the rug if you're upset; this is especially true for parents and stepparents. At the end of the day, you don't want to upset your parent or stepparent, but being consistent and following through with consequences after boundaries are crossed is essential. It may be the push your loved one needs to understand you mean business.

Furthermore, remember that boundaries are in place to protect others from feeling uncomfortable as well. Respect boundaries that others give you, and respect your stepparent if they confide in you or choose to give you advice that you've asked for. Remember to appreciate their time and care when helping you. This will help establish a mutual respect for one another that can be nurtured for the rest of your life with your stepparent. Another way to maintain mutual respect is by being respectful in your language with your stepparent. Watch yourself with offensive language and if you do offend them, apologize.

Sometimes we all need to take a step back and understand that we're all human. That includes your parents and stepparents too. Foster understanding and empathy, and above all else, give them the benefit of the doubt when you can.

Chapter Seven

Socializing with Your Stepparent

In this chapter, we delve into the art of maintaining a rich and rewarding relationship with your parents as an adult. Communication is different as you transition, so therefore, being social with them is also different. This is a time when you and your parents can finally be on some equal footing and grow your relationship beyond that of a parent-child relationship. It's a time to get to know them for them and maintain the bond you'll have for the rest of your lives.

Call Them

Regular communication is the cornerstone of any healthy relationship. In the hustle and bustle of adult life, it's easy to lose touch with the people who matter most. To bridge the gap, pick up the phone and call your stepparent as regularly as you can. When you can't, text them.

A simple "How are you?" can do wonders, and an even more in-depth conversation about your lives can strengthen and maintain the bond you have with your family. Frequent communication is an expression of your love and care. It assures your stepparent that they are an important part of your life and that you value them and choose them as a priority.

Keep in mind that keeping in touch is not only about sharing your experiences but also about staying updated on theirs. Hearing about their daily activities, their future goals, and their achievements and struggles creates a deeper understanding of them as people. It also gives you a chance to empathize with them and truly walk in their shoes. Ultimately, our stepparents likely didn't tell us everything initially—but now you have a chance to truly engage with them on equal footing, which can strengthen the bond you have with them. Conversations over the phone can be as comforting as a warm hug, creating a sense of closeness even when physical distances separate you.

Another aspect of reaching out is showing them that you're being proactive and choosing them. That can make it easier for them to initiate contact in the future.

Let Them Confide in You

Your stepparent may have played the role of protector, mentor, and confidant for a good chunk of your life. Or maybe they didn't because they've just come along recently. Regardless, as you mature into adulthood, you have the opportunity to be that for them just as much as they can be that for you.

Create a space where your stepparent feels safe to confide in you, sharing their thoughts, joys, and even their concerns or fears. Your role as a caring and attentive listener can offer them much-needed emotional support. Be their friend. Be their family. Be their shoulder to lean on if they want you to be.

Allowing your stepparent to open up to you is not a one-sided exchange; it's a mutually beneficial process. Their ability to share their experiences, feelings, and wisdom provides you with an opportunity to learn and grow. By encouraging their confidences, you create a deeper level of intimacy, respect, and understanding in your relationship. This can foster a sense of mutual trust and reinforce the idea that you're there for each other, as family should be, no matter the circumstances.

If your stepparent does choose to confide in you, be sure to exercise the patience and empathy you'd expect them to give you if the roles were reversed. Even if their concerns might seem trivial or irrelevant at the moment, remember that their emotions are real and significant, and there were probably times that your issues seemed trivial to others, too. By offering a listening ear and a shoulder to lean on, you're giving them a valuable gift: the assurance that their thoughts and feelings matter.

Show Physical Admiration and Affection

Physical touch is a universal language of affection, and as we touched on earlier, it may very well be your stepparent's love language. It's a great way to express emotions and convey love and appreciation. In fact, one of the simplest yet most profound ways to convey your feelings is by giving your stepparent a warm, heartfelt hug as soon as you see them.

Hugs are not just gestures of greeting; they can be symbols of love, acceptance, and reassurance. When you embrace your stepparent, you're telling them that you're grateful for them and their presence, that you cherish the time you have together, and that you're genuinely pleased to see them. These sentiments can go a long way, especially for a stepparent who may not always feel accepted from the get-go.

The act of hugging can release oxytocin, which is similar to endorphins and serotonin and commonly referred to as the "love hormone." It has the power to reduce stress and anxiety, lower blood pressure, and create a sense of emotional connection. In this way, hugging your stepparent not only communicates love and appreciation but also brings about physiological benefits, reinforcing the importance of physical contact in maintaining a strong bond.

Get Together for the Holidays

Holidays offer the perfect occasion for family reunions and the opportunity to celebrate the bond you share with your loved ones. Whether it's the traditional holidays like Thanksgiving, Christmas, New Year's, or more unique family celebrations, coming together during these special moments strengthens your familial ties. Now, if you have a blended family or multiple family members you feel obligated to visit, this can be challenging.

Sometimes as families age, people can start to move away or drift apart. It may be difficult as the family tree branches out to get together on the bigger holidays. It may also be difficult if there's no way to mix company with certain family members, especially when that has to do with negative emotions or feelings surrounding your stepparent and their relationship with your biological parent.

However, by creating or just revamping your family traditions and rituals, you can still figure out ways to get together with everyone equally (if that's what you want). For instance, it's okay to deviate from the typical holidays. Consider spending alternating holidays between parents (or near the holidays), but a great way to deviate from the holidays is by establishing annual holidays of your own!

Consider an annual family picnic or a "family day" where you engage in various activities together. These don't have to be near or on big holidays. Many families choose to do these sorts of events on nice, warm weather days so the kids can be outside playing and the adults get a chance to soak in some Vitamin D and enjoy time together. This may be difficult to plan weather-wise. If you want it to be on the same day annually, choose a time when the weather is generally mild, and have indoor and outdoor activities in mind!

These traditions build a sense of togetherness and make your relationship with your entire family feel more special and distinctive.

Additionally, taking the time to prepare and enjoy meals together during the holidays or family events can be a deeply bonding experience. Cooking together, sharing recipes, and savoring all of the dishes you've prepared together can create cherished memories for many years to come.

Let Your Kids Call Them "Grandma" or "Grandpa"

This is a touchy subject for some families. Obviously, this guide is not a one-size-fits-all, but if you're looking at expanding your relationship with your stepparent and you have children, consider letting your kids call them "grandma" or "grandpa." This comes with a few caveats. For one thing, if they are new to the picture and your children are older, they may have a difficult time calling them that.

If your stepparent has been in the picture for a while, let your kids and your stepparent choose what they are to be called. If you struggle calling them "mom" or "dad," that's okay! What you call your stepparent doesn't have to mirror what your kids call them. If your children are comfortable or see them as a grandparent, let them call them by those sorts of names, even if you don't refer to them as your mom or dad. If your children have been raised with them participating actively in their lives, and your stepparent and children are all on board, definitely let them call them these endearing terms.

Your children may learn to call them this on their own accord, depending on what the family dynamic looks like. Avoid correcting your children in a matter such as this. It can lead to negative feelings and emotions surrounding the dynamic when it had been positive. At the end of the day, it isn't about you; it's about your child and their relationship with your stepparent. As long as your children are loved and have a healthy relationship with your stepparent, do not steer them away from calling your stepparent whatever seems natural. This will help your child develop more positive adult relationships (which is essential for development and growth) and allow your stepparent the opportunity to feel included and loved.

Take Them Out

Don't forget to treat your stepparent from time to time. If you appreciate them and are looking at more ways to grow your relationship, ask them to go out with you from time to time. You can set appropriate boundaries if there are struggles within your relationship, or even if there are no issues at all. The boundaries you can set for going out with your stepparent include:

- Who pays

- How often you go out together

- If you go out one-on-one for bonding

Laugh Together

Have a sense of humor even if everything isn't always fun or funny. Don't think that you have to create a perfect image of a blended family. Things will happen how they're supposed to given proper boundaries, love, and nurturing, but not everything will run smoothly all the time. The more you can laugh—at the situation and with your stepparent and the rest of your family—the faster everyone will adjust in a positive way. Don't be afraid to have fun or let loose. Life is all about experiences. Why not experience a little more joy? And if you can include your stepparent in that, why wouldn't you?

Take Them on Family Vacations

This may not be the easiest thing for several different reasons. For one, if there's animosity between your parents, it could feel like you're stuck in the middle choosing who goes on vacation with you, especially when these are extravagant vacations. If this is the case, you may want to start doing vacations on a smaller scale and try to include everyone on an alternating basis. However, if someone makes you feel guilty for inviting your stepparent on a family vacation when you want to strengthen and maintain that relationship, communication is in order. You need to communicate your boundaries and your need for a relationship with that stepparent. Do not allow toxic opinions to dictate your relationships.

The second reason this may be difficult is traveling with family in general as an adult can be stressful. However, understand that introducing your parents—including your stepparent—to travel can be an incredibly rewarding and enriching experience. It's a chance to create cherished memories across the globe and discover completely unchartered territory together. This not only strengthens your familial bond but helps you all grow individually in your journey.

Traveling abroad may take careful planning, but it is an opportunity to open the door to other cultures or ideals that you may not experience regularly. It is important that we take essential steps and strategies for a fun time for everyone. This is everything from choosing the right destination to striking the perfect balance between new experiences and comfortable ones.

Choose Locations Carefully: Getting your folks on board is often as simple as finding out where they want to go. However, it's not always as easy as asking them, especially if they're the type to go with the flow or who wants to please everyone. If they are like that, it may be up to you to come up with something, and in order to do that, think about what they might enjoy. Maybe they're history buffs with a special interest in World War II. Maybe they love going to the theater together. Or, maybe their ancestors came from another country, a country they may want to visit. Have they ever mentioned something like an African safari or seeing Egyptian pyramids? Try to find some interests and go from there!

Pick an "Easier" Location If Need Be: Baby steps are usually a good idea with novice travelers of any age. A DIY trip through India, for instance, might be a more challenging adventure for many travelers, and it may be better to start small.

Instead, opt for a place without a language barrier. For those who aren't quite as adventurous, potentially look at places with familiar foods. The fewer things that are likely to push your parent and stepparent out of their comfort zone, the more likely they may be to try something new along the way.

Cruises can be a good option. That is because they cater to a multitude of different people at any given time. Also, your parent and stepparent can enjoy excursions and adventure during the day, and then come back to the familiarity of the ship afterward. This option can also help when dealing with finances because a majority of the expenses are paid beforehand.

Start Slow: As stated, baby steps. Although you may not think it's worth the long flight for a trip that's shorter than two weeks, if your parent and/or stepparent are embarking on their first international trip, you should probably start with something shorter. A five-to-seven-day trip in one place with a day trip or two may be a better option unless you have a particularly adventurous parent and/or stepparent. Think of it like the sampler platter at a new restaurant you go to—they'll get to try a few things so that they know better what suits them for the next time. This is great because it prevents them from being completely overwhelmed by too much all at once.

Determine the Budget and Finances Ahead of Time: Are you fronting the entire bill for this? If not, it's definitely worth talking about beforehand. As awkward as discussions about money can be with your family, they're still necessary to have before a big trip. If you want to treat them to an international trip, that's wonderful—but if you're not paying for everything, it's critical to make sure they know that and to ensure that they can afford the trip. Decide before you book anything who is paying for what!

Don't Over-Schedule Your Days: Even if you don't think you're a fast-paced traveler, chances are good that you'd pack more into a day than your parent and stepparent might have done on their own. Travel can be overwhelming and exhausting even when it's great.

Remember that everyone benefits from being well-rested. No one wants to vacation with someone who's grouchy because they're tired or hungry!

If you're touring a museum or doing something strenuous in the morning, leave the afternoon open. If you've got plans to have a late dinner and see a show, allow for sleeping in or naps (or both) earlier in the day. Make sure everyone is well-fed and well-rested.

It's also important to note any mobility issues your parent and/or stepparent may have. Even if they're still spry, spending a whole day walking on cobblestone streets can be hard on joints. Consider their regular schedule at home and how much more active you'll all be when traveling, and plan accordingly.

Get Everyone Involved: This is the one time that you can't just let someone say, "Whatever you want to do is fine!" Make sure everyone going on your trip has input and talks about what they want to do. Top priorities need to be included in the itinerary.

No matter what you have to do, get the feedback, even if you have to initiate every planning session or if you have to send them links to articles or drop off guide books to them. Make sure they look, research, and let you know anything they'd like to do. This alleviates surprises during the trip and also makes everyone feel represented!

Plan as Much as Possible in Advance: Whether or not you're the type of traveler who plans ahead, it's an important thing to keep in mind when taking your parent and stepparent on any trip, especially one abroad.

It will mean less wasted time during the trip going back and forth on the topic of what to do every day. It means booking skip-the-line tours, so no one has to stand for hours outside any given attraction. It means everyone knows (and approves of) the itinerary in advance and isn't surprised last minute with something they don't want to do.

Balance New Experiences with Comfortable Ones: For many of us, learning and experiencing new things is one of the biggest perks of traveling. That doesn't have to change when you bring your family along for the ride, even if they're a bit less adventurous than you are. It is likely that you have a good sense of your parent's or stepparent's comfort zones and what might be pushing it too far.

Find ways to make sure they're not spending too much time being uncomfortable. This can be achieved by proper balance. Go out to eat that adventurous meal for lunch and opt for a more familiar dinner. And on the flip side, if they're more adventurous than you are, be open to trying things but make sure they opt for something a little milder afterward. You never know, they may push you to do something you might not have done otherwise. Balance makes sure that all of you are happy!

Plan Some Alone Time: This may sound counter-intuitive to going on a vacation with your parent and stepparent, but it is a good idea to carve out a little alone time—especially if you're also going with your partner. See if they wouldn't mind doing one activity while you and your spouse do another. Or maybe you guys want to hang back while they go to that museum down the street. Either way, just plan one or two things during the trip that you can do on your own (or with your partner).

This is particularly important if you live a bit further away from your parent and stepparent and haven't spent a lot of time with them in recent years. Even during a week-long trip, you may want to plan a day in the middle where you all get a break from one another. After all, everyone needs a chance to reset their clock. This is especially true if there are CDs in the mix.

Keep Everyone in Mind: This may be the most important—and most difficult—thing to do. You worked hard for those vacation days and saved up to go on this trip, and the last thing you want is to come home disappointed. When you decide to introduce international travel (or even domestic travel) to your folks, you're signing on to take them on a trip that suits them as well.

Depending on your parent and stepparent, that might mean hotels instead of hostels, taxis instead of walking, museums instead of nightclubs, and more sit-down restaurants than street food. The perfect trip is out there for both you and them. And you never know, they may just surprise you with how much adventure they're willing to have!

Plan Game Nights and Family Get-Togethers with Them

When you sit down to play a game with your family, you are building relationships, making space for important conversations, practicing all-important social skills, working on brain and strategy skills, and, probably most importantly, you're making memories.

If game nights have always been a part of your family's culture, it may not seem like that hundredth run of Monopoly is important, but it is. You are building something larger, something that you can't see right now, but it exists!

It's also necessary to help your stepparent feel welcome (whether you had game nights as a child or not) and continually including them in this will solidify your relationship. So, play! Enjoy each other! Make memories! Remember that just because you plan game nights with one biological parent and your stepparent doesn't mean you can't do the same with the other parent (and your other stepparent if both of your natural parents are remarried). Experiment with times that work for everyone, and if you can't do two game nights a week, a month, etc., consider alternating to every other one to make time for everyone!

Schedule a Time That Works for Everyone: The term "family game night" means the family is involved, but it doesn't have to mean "night." Schedule a time that works best for you and your family. Whenever there's downtime, you should schedule your game time. Just make sure you set a day and a time that works for all members of your family and then try to stick to it.

Consistency will mean the most in this. If a weekly game night is too overwhelming, try something monthly first (and as mentioned earlier, if you're alternating with other family members, do each every other month)!

It's not supposed to feel like a chore, but it should require a bit of sacrifice. It doesn't matter when or how often; just you pick something that works so you can stick to it.

Pick More Than One Game: Have a few games in mind for any given night. Some families may have a few favorites they want to play every time, while others may want to keep a rotation of a few tried and true. Keep it fun and fresh with a few curveballs from time to time. And then some families prefer a new game every single time. Consider rotating who picks the game or brings it, or possibly setting up a subscription that sends new games every month. Whatever you decide, make sure everyone is on board, and that it's appropriate and easy enough for everyone who intends to play.

Do Not Disturb: Set your phone to Do Not Disturb mode. Having technology at your fingertips is wonderful but you don't need it for game night (unless you choose to incorporate video games into your game nights). Turn off televisions and other distractions as well. This is a time for family!

Make Sure There's Food: Everyone loves food. Everyone loves drinks. Make sure you have plenty planned whether it's takeout, something you cook, or provided by you and/or your family members. Every time there's a game night planned, make sure food is involved.

Remember to Have Fun: It's easy to get wrapped up in everyday life. It's even easier to let it affect your mood when you spend time with your family. But don't let it! This is a time for you and yours, so enjoy each other and remember that real life will be there when you're finished with your time together. Game nights should be fun and stress-free, even if the game itself is new and challenging. Try to relax and be mindful of the moment and know that you're creating memories that can last a lifetime!

Be Patient: If you're the type to be overly competitive, make sure you're being patient with those who may need a bit more time to understand the game. Be patient with children who may argue, and just explain to them calmly that it's a game, and that you're all learning and trying to have fun together. Understand that all game nights won't be perfect, and don't let your expectations ruin the good nature of the evening. Kids will argue. Tears may happen for our more sensitive family members. Accusations of cheating may be flow. There may also be sore winners or sore losers. Whatever the case, just remember that you and your family are together, and you're playing. Use these times as teachable moments for you and your family, and discuss ways to improve.

Thank Everyone for Coming: This may sound silly, but when everyone is finished playing, thank them. Thank them for coming, thank them for playing, and thank them for interacting with one another. Tell them you had fun playing with them, and that you're looking forward to the next game night.

Plan the Next One: Even if you have the same day and time in place for every game night, make sure you plan the next one. This can be as simple as confirming everyone will be there at the day and time agreed upon or asking what you're having for dinner that night. Just make sure that you plan it and that everyone has it locked into their calendars so they don't forget.

Revisit Places of Significance

Revisiting places that are important to you is often an emotional experience, but revisiting a place that is important to both you and your stepparent is some of the best medicine you can give to your relationship together.

These places are part of your shared life together, and revisiting them reinforces the idea that you've all built something meaningful over time; a true family unit. Reliving positive experiences can be beneficial to both of you and your respective mental health. Make the most out of revisiting by:

- Plan Together: Discuss which places hold the most meaning for each of you. It could be the place where your parent and stepparent first met or fell in love; a place where you had your first family vacation or getaway after they got married; the town you moved to when they moved in together; a baseball field you grew up going to; the first outing they took you to; or anything that holds significance to you both.

- Schedule Visits: Make plans to visit these kinds of places periodically. You can schedule a day trip or weekend getaway to spend quality time there. Consider making these sorts of revisits part of an anniversary tradition or ritual.

- Create New Memories: Don't always rely on your nostalgia to get you through. When you go back to this special place, make sure you're trying to create new memories together there.

- Share Reflections: Talk about your feelings and memories associated with these places. This is a great bonding exercise.

- Stay Present: While revisiting, stay present in the moment. Put away your cell phone and focus on only each other.

Key Takeaways

Chapter 7: Socializing with Your Stepparent focuses on nurturing and enriching the relationship with your stepparent as an adult and how to use your social needs to get closer to them. It emphasizes the transition in your familial dynamics as you grow and journey through your own life and highlights various ways to build and sustain a strong bond with your stepparent through social interactions. Best practices in socializing with your parents include these factors.

Maintain Regular Communication: Keep in touch consistently through calls or texts. Show interest in their lives, which includes all of their achievements, struggles, and aspirations. Engage in meaningful conversations that allow for understanding and closeness, and show that they are a priority by reaching out often.

Provide Emotional Support: Create a safe space for your stepparent to confide in you. Be a caring listener by offering empathy and understanding as often as you can. Encourage open communication to strengthen mutual trust and respect.

Express Affection: Physical touch such as hugs can convey love, acceptance, and appreciation, which can be pivotal in a relationship with your stepparent due to the negative stigma that often comes with being a stepparent and the feeling of not belonging. These gestures contribute to emotional bonding and can reduce stress, which can in turn grow and strengthen your bond.

Celebrate Holidays and Create Traditions: Find ways to celebrate holidays or create your own family traditions. It's an opportunity to bond and strengthen relationships, even if you have a blended family or complex dynamics.

Accept New Family Dynamics: Allow your children to choose what they call your stepparent. Make sure that you're being a ray of positive light when it comes to that and allow for them to each feel included and loved in their very own relationship.

Quality Time Together: Arrange outings, treat them to experiences, and laugh together. Foster a sense of humor and joy in your interactions, allowing everyone to relax and enjoy each other's company.

Travel Together: Introducing your stepparent to travel can be rewarding. Plan trips with consideration for their preferences and comfort, ensuring a balance between new experiences and familiarity.

Plan Family Activities and Game Nights: Engage in family activities such as game nights to build relationships, make memories, and strengthen connections.

Revisit Meaningful Places: Revisiting places of significance can evoke shared memories, reinforce bonds, and create new experiences together.

By incorporating these practices into your relationship with your stepparent, you can cultivate a deeper, more meaningful connection that lasts a lifetime, transitioning from a parent-child relationship to one built on mutual respect, love, and understanding.

Chapter Eight
Final Thoughts

As we conclude this journey exploring the myriad ways to cultivate and nurture a loving relationship with your stepparent, it's crucial to reflect on the profound significance of these connections in our lives. What does your stepparent bring to the table? Do their emotional strengths complement yours and the rest of your family's?

The very fact that you have picked up this book means that you have some sort of motivation or desire to strengthen your relationship. Perhaps you can start by learning to lean on them for support and companionship. The complexities of stepfamily dynamics often require patience, understanding, and an unwavering commitment to not only establish but maintain genuine bonds. There can also be dynamics that have a lot of negativity intertwined within them, and it's important not to let those negative emotions latch on. Instead, breathe nothing but positivity into your relationship with your stepparent.

Above Everything Else, Communicate

Throughout this book, we've delved into the depths of understanding personality types—highlighting the contrasting traits of the Cave Dweller (CD) and the Mountain Yeller (MY). Recognizing these differences isn't merely a means of classification but a pathway toward empathy. It allows us the opportunity to comprehend and appreciate the varying perspectives that each member of our family has and shape our interactions with them.

If you take nothing else from this guidebook, take the importance of communication. Communication emerges as the cornerstone of any thriving and healthy relationship. We've emphasized the importance of expressing feelings without igniting conflicts, the art of active listening, and the power of employing neutral language to foster an environment free from defensiveness. This is especially true when engaging with a stepparent. Blended families often have sensitivities, and it's essential to learn how to communicate with one another.

Setting clear expectations and being open about family dynamics lays the groundwork for building trust and understanding within the unit. So set clear expectations and boundaries, and above all else, show your stepparent that you love and appreciate them the best way you can—using this guide to help you show that love.

After all, with love comes attachment. Strong attachment bonds set us apart from other animals and allow us to socialize through life with others. Your stepparent didn't have to be there from birth or through the majority of your childhood, either. What matters is the attachment you have with them and the one you can grow through mutual respect, understanding, communication, and yes—love.

We Are All Human

As we discussed in this guide, a funny thing happens when you become an adult. You finally start to realize that your parents are real humans, and they are quite a lot less than perfect—and this includes your stepparent. You're not a kid anymore, sure, but that doesn't mean that there won't always be challenges in your relationship with your parents—and your stepparent, for that matter. Family is family, and there will always be an opportunity for conflict as long as there is an opportunity for growth. Make sure that you continue to give them the benefit of the doubt, love them despite their flaws, and understand that they are likely doing their best at any given moment.

They make mistakes, just as you do, and you have to understand that you must set your expectations to a realistic standard. You also need to put your relationship with your stepparent to a realistic standard. Nurturing your bond every single day is important, but it isn't very realistic the older we get. As life's obligations pile up, loving your stepparent can quickly fall to the bottom of the to-do list. This is okay!

Make sure you're picking it back up as often as you can, and still communicating and expressing your love for one another. It doesn't have to entail grandeur or extravagance. Sometimes it can be a small text message that says, "Thinking of you."

Prioritizing time together—truly quality time—will ensure that your stepparent feels heard, understood, accepted, and loved. Mix that with small acts or gestures of surprise and kindness, and you can truly build a strong foundation that won't be harmed by a missed day or thirty of communication.

Respect Differences

Ultimately, navigating these family roles takes time, practice, and lots of communication and effort. You likely knew when you were younger that you and your parents were not the same people, so it's incredibly important in adulthood to continue that mentality. It is even more true of your stepparent.

Your stepparent likely has different priorities, values, or goals than you do. They likely also have different opinions on how to parent or carry one's self as an adult citizen. That's perfectly okay! They don't have to agree with you, and you don't have to agree with them. But take responsibility for the fact that it is also up to you to navigate these situations with dignity and respect.

In fact, if you treat these differences with the respect that they deserve, your parent and stepparent are likely much more receptive to your perspective. You can be honest about who you are and what's important to you without being dismissive of their beliefs. Let's take a look at some other strategies for communicating this respect and building a healthier relationship with your parents.

Take Responsibility

If you want to set boundaries in your adult relationship with your parent and stepparent, then it is important that you not act like a child in the process. Respect their boundaries. Respect their opinions. Respect their differences. Above all else, if you want to be treated as an adult and respected as an adult, make sure that you're not playing both sides of the fiddle.

Avoid asking them to do things for you that you don't truly need them to do. They no longer should feel financially or physically responsible for you, and you should no longer ask them to do things for you that you can do for yourself. However, keep in mind that if you do need help, don't be afraid to ask. We all need help from time to time, but when you take advantage and ask your family for help when you don't need it, you're only setting yourself and your boundaries up for failure.

The truth is that your parent and stepparent are more likely to treat you like an adult if you act like one. For example, you might feel tempted to call them to complain every time you argue with your partner—or you can ask to borrow money when you need extra cash, knowing that you just spent your money on items or services you didn't necessarily need. Remember, just because something is an easy solution doesn't mean that it's good for you or your relationship. The more responsibility you can take for yourself and your own decisions, the more your parents and stepparent will treat you like an adult.

Stop Making Assumptions

Conflicts can quickly erupt in families because people make assumptions about what someone wants or how they will react to any given situation. For example, you shouldn't assume your stepparent doesn't have plans and will drop everything to do something with you when you ask. Likewise, even if something is a "usual" thing for you and your stepparent, don't assume that they can make it every time. For example, if the two of you have gotten into a routine of going out for brunch every Sunday, don't assume that's a tradition that can't be broken just because it's something the two of you have been doing regularly. Have that conversation and remember that relationships are two-way streets.

Both of you have to agree to something before it's written in stone. You should respect their time just as you expect them to respect yours. Instead, share your desire to spend time together and communicate what you'd like to accomplish. This will make your relationship with your stepparent a lot easier to navigate in the future and give you both the opportunity to grow and develop the relationship accordingly.

Stay in Contact and Practice Being Present—Even When There's Conflict

Being around each other every day is likely not going to happen with you and your stepparent unless you live in the same home, but when you are together, make sure that you're being present. Being truly present in another person's life means involving yourself in their hopes, dreams, accomplishments, and everything in between. It also means showing genuine care and empathy when they face challenges. And this is all for better or worse.

Loving someone is a choice you have to make every day. When things are tense with a parent or stepparent, it can be all too easy to not return a phone call or to just leave them on "read" in your text thread. You may be thinking that as an adult, you're free to cut off contact whenever you feel like it, unlike when you were a kid, and likely couldn't escape them even if you wanted to. However, it is important to note that unless a relationship is abusive or toxic to your mental health, you should never cut off contact. Avoiding them may feel like the appropriate choice in the moment, and it may honestly feel therapeutic, but it's not wise. Not only are you cheating yourself out of an opportunity to grow and mature as a human by facing the conflict, but you're also harming your relationship by damaging the trust.

Trust is everything in a relationship, no matter what kind. So, continue to choose to love your stepparent even through disagreements. You can take a moment to breathe and take a step back to assess your emotions and feelings when arguments or disagreements arise, but always promise to come back to the discussion at another time. Your relationship depends on consistency and effort. So choose to love your stepparent, and make that conscious choice every day to show them that you're worthy of their trust, their respect, and their affection.

Appendices

Self-Assessment Questionnaire: Determine if You're a CD, MY, or Straddler

In the quest for self-understanding, recognizing one's intrinsic personality traits plays a crucial role. This self-assessment questionnaire has been carefully designed to help you discern whether you align most closely with the introspective nature of a Cave Dweller (CD), the extroverted inclinations of a Mountain Yeller (MY), or the balanced characteristics of a Straddler. By reflecting on your behaviors, preferences, and reactions in various situations, this tool aims to provide insight into your predominant personality type. Approach each question with honesty and openness, and remember, there's no right or wrong answer – just a deeper understanding of your unique self waiting to be unveiled.

Personality Indicator #1

Circle one answer per question.

1. Have you ever walked in your sleep during your adult life?

    YES or NO

2. As a teenager, did you feel comfortable expressing your feelings to one or both of your parents?

YES or NO

3. Do you tend to look directly into a person's eyes when talking to them?

YES or NO

4. Do you feel that most people, when you first meet them, are uncritical of your appearance?

YES or NO

5. In a group situation with people you've just met, would you feel comfortable drawing attention to yourself by initiating a conversation?

YES or NO

6. Do you feel comfortable holding hands or hugging someone you're in a relationship with in front of other people?

YES or NO

7. When someone talks about feeling warm physically, do you begin to feel warm also?

YES or NO

8. Do you tend to tune out when someone is talking to you because you're anxious to come up with your side of the story?

YES or NO

9. Do you feel that you learn better by seeing and/or reading than by hearing?

YES or NO

10. In a new class or company meeting, do you usually feel comfortable asking questions in front of the group?

YES or NO

11. When expressing your ideas, do you find it important to relate all the details leading up to the subject so the other person can understand it completely?

YES or NO

12. Do you enjoy relating to children?

YES or NO

13. Are you comfortable with your body movements when faced with unfamiliar people and circumstances?

YES or NO

14. Do you prefer reading fiction rather than non-fiction?

YES or NO

15. If you were to imagine sucking on a juicy lemon, would your mouth water?

YES or NO

16. Do you feel comfortable receiving a compliment in front of other people?

YES or NO

17. Do you feel that you're a good conversationalist?

YES or NO

18. Do you feel comfortable when complimentary attention is drawn to your physical body?

YES or NO

Personality Indicator # 2

Circle one answer per question.

1. Have you ever awakened in the middle of the night and felt that you could not move your body and/or talk?

YES or NO

2. As a child, did you feel you were more affected by your parent's tone of voice than by what they actually said?

YES or NO

3. If someone you know talks about a fear that you've experienced before, do you tend to re-experience that apprehension or fear?

YES or NO

4. After arguing with someone, do you tend to dwell on what you could or should have said?

YES or NO

5. Do you tend to occasionally tune out when someone is talking to you and therefore don't hear what's being said because your mind drifts to something totally unrelated?

YES or NO

6. Do you sometimes desire to be complimented for a job well done, but feel embarrassed or uncomfortable when complemented?

YES or NO

7. Do you often fear not being able to carry on a conversation with someone you've just met?

YES or NO

8. Do you feel self-conscious when attention is drawn to your physical body or appearance?

YES or NO

9. If you had a choice, would you rather avoid being around children most of the time?

YES or NO

10. Do you feel uptight in body movements, especially when faced with unfamiliar people or circumstances?

YES or NO

11. Do you prefer reading non-fiction rather than fiction?

YES or NO

12. If someone describes a very bitter taste, do you have difficulty experiencing the physical feeling of that bitter taste?

YES or NO

13. Do you generally feel that you see yourself less favorably than others see you?

YES or NO

14. Do you tend to feel awkward or self-conscious holding hands and/or kissing someone you're in a relationship with in front of other people?

YES or NO

15. In a new lecture or company meeting, do you usually feel uncomfortable asking questions in front of the group?

YES or NO

16. Do you feel uneasy if someone you've just met looks you directly in the eyes when talking to you, especially if the conversation is about you?

YES or NO

17. In a group situation with people you've just met, would you

feel uncomfortable drawing attention to yourself by initiating a conversation?

YES or NO

18. If you're in a relationship or are very close to someone, do you find it difficult or embarrassing to verbalize your love for them?

YES or NO

Personality Indicator Scores

Personality Indicator #1

- Give yourself 10 points for every *yes* answer for questions one and two.
- Give yourself 5 points for every answer for questions three through eighteen.
- Write the total number at the top of #1's questionnaire.

Personality Indicator #2

- Give yourself 10 points for every *yes* answer for questions one and two.
- Give yourself 5 points for every answer for questions three through eighteen.
- Write the total number at the top of #2's questionnaire.
- Combine the total from PI 1 & 2.

Using the Scoring Chart

On the scoring chart, look up the combined score of Personality Indicator 1 & 2 on the HORIZONTAL axis of the chart, and circle the number.

- Take the total score of PI #1 and locate it on the VERTICAL axis of the chart, and circle the number.

- Draw a horizontal line across the page from the PI 1 score and a vertical line down from the combined score.

- The number in the box where the two lines intersect represents your true, adjusted percentage personality indicator.

- Scores 61 and higher indicate a Mountain Yeller personality type.

- Scores 45 and lower indicate a Cave Dweller personality type.

- Scores 47 to 56 indicate a Straddler personality type.

Cave Dweller Tendencies

- Reserved
- Head-ruled
- Controlling
- Wants space and security
- Prefers socializing one-on-one
- Singular focus
- Thinks before reacting

- Prefers showing affection privately
- Distrusts flattery
- Enjoys working alone
- Enjoys individual activities
- Wants alone time
- Dresses for comfort
- Decides after thinking about it
- Speaks literally, to the point
- Infers from what others say
- Feels emotional pain in the mind
- Fears loss of security

Cave Dweller Priorities

- Career/financial security
- Hobbies/children
- Relationships/family
- Sex/lovers

Mountain Yeller Tendencies

- Outgoing

- Heart-ruled
- Dominating
- Wants connection and touch
- Enjoys socializing in groups
- Moving focus
- Reacts spontaneously
- Comfortable with affection anytime
- Likes reassurance and compliments
- Enjoys working with people
- Enjoys team activities
- Wants to be together as much as possible
- Decides in the moment
- Speaks inferentially—adds story
- Takes what others say literally
- Feels emotional pain in body and mind
- Fears rejection

Mountain Yeller Priorities

- Relationships/sex
- Family/children

- Friends/hobbies

- Career/financial security

COMBINED SCORE #1 AND #2

SCORE #1 \ Combined	50	55	60	65	70	75	80	85	90	95	100	105	110	115	120	125	130	135	140	145	150	155	160	165	170	175	180	185	190	195	200
100											100	95	91	87	83	80	77	74	71	69	67	65	63	61	59	57	56	54	53	51	50
95										100	95	90	86	83	79	76	73	70	68	66	63	61	59	58	56	54	53	51	50	49	48
90									100	95	90	86	82	78	75	72	69	67	64	62	60	58	56	55	53	51	50	49	47	46	45
85								100	94	89	85	81	77	74	71	68	65	63	61	59	57	55	53	52	50	49	47	46	45	44	43
80							100	94	89	84	80	76	73	70	67	64	62	58	57	56	53	52	50	48	47	46	44	43	42	41	40
75						100	94	88	83	79	75	71	68	65	63	60	58	56	54	52	50	48	47	45	44	43	42	41	39	38	38
70					100	93	88	82	78	74	70	67	64	61	58	56	54	52	50	48	47	45	44	42	41	40	39	38	37	36	35
65				100	93	87	81	76	72	68	65	62	59	57	54	52	50	48	46	45	43	42	41	39	38	37	36	35	34	33	33
60			100	92	86	80	75	71	67	63	60	57	55	52	50	48	46	44	43	41	40	39	38	36	35	34	33	32	32	31	30
55		100	92	85	79	73	69	65	61	58	56	52	50	48	46	44	42	41	39	38	37	35	34	33	32	31	31	30	29	28	28
50	100	91	83	77	71	67	63	59	56	53	50	48	45	43	42	40	38	37	36	34	33	32	31	30	29	28	28	27	26	26	25
45	90	82	75	69	64	60	56	53	50	47	45	43	41	39	38	36	35	33	32	31	30	29	28	27	26	26	25	24	24	23	23
40	80	73	67	62	57	53	50	47	44	42	40	38	36	35	33	32	31	30	29	28	27	26	25	24	24	23	22	22	21	21	20
35	70	64	58	54	50	47	44	41	39	37	35	33	32	30	29	28	27	26	25	24	23	23	22	21	21	20	19	19	18	18	18
30	60	55	50	46	43	40	38	35	33	32	30	29	27	26	25	24	23	22	21	21	20	19	19	18	18	17	17	16	16	15	15
25	50	46	42	38	36	33	31	29	28	26	25	24	23	22	21	20	19	19	18	17	17	16	16	15	15	14	14	14	13	13	13
20	40	36	33	31	29	27	26	24	22	21	20	19	18	17	17	16	15	15	14	14	13	13	13	12	12	11	11	11	11	10	10
15	30	27	25	23	21	20	19	18	17	16	15	14	13	13	12	12	11	11	10	10	10	9	9	9	9	8	8	8	8	8	8
10	20	18	17	15	14	13	13	12	11	11	10	10	9	9	8	8	8	7	7	7	7	6	6	6	6	6	5	5	5	5	5
5	10	9	8	8	7	7	6	6	6	5	5	5	5	4	4	4	4	4	3	3	3	3	3	3	3	3	3	3	3	3	3
0	0	0	0	0	0	0	0	0	0	0	0	0	0	0	0	0	0	0	0	0	0	0	0	0	0	0	0	0	0	0	0

www.ingramcontent.com/pod-product-compliance
Lightning Source LLC
Chambersburg PA
CBHW070115080526
44586CB00013B/1301